Neil's War

To
Wing Commander W. M. Russell DFC and Bar
1909-1944
And to his fellow crew members on Halifax LL 280 of
138 Squadron shot down over occupied France on
May 8th, 1944.

Neil's War

One boy's story of his evacuation to Ireland
at the outbreak of WWII

Neil W. Murphy

RoseTintedSpecs Imprint

In telling the story **Neil's War** the author has endeavoured to
portray as accurately as possible people, places and events in the
period 1939 to 1944. Any similarity between characters in this
book and real persons, living or dead is purely coincidental, Neil
Murphy Ltd.

Cover images "Grant's Department Store Fire, 1942" by kind
permission of the Irish Examiner; "Sinking of the SS Irish
Oak" by kind permission of Kenneth King and the National
Maritime Museum of Ireland; "Lancaster Bomber" courtesy of
Rose Photo Archive; "Michael, Jean and Neil" courtesy of the
author.
Font licensing correct at time of publication. British English
spelling is used in this book.

ISBN 978-0-9544518-5-1

RoseTintedSpecs Imprint
Publisher: David Rose
PO Box 209, Whitstable CT5 2WD, United Kingdom
www.rosetintedspecs.com
email: publisher@rosetintedspecs.com

Copies of this book can be purchased through the company's
web site. Printed in the USA and UK

Contents

Acknowledgements vi

Preface vii

Chapters One to Fifteen 13-275

Epilogue 277

Author's Notes 283

Acknowledgements

I was about to delete the document "Neil's War" prior to disposing of my old computer when I remembered my sister Rose asking about the story a couple of months earlier. I e-mailed it to her at RoseTintedSpecs Imprint. Their response was immediate, "it's a classic."

Well, this is hard to ignore! Heartened by their suggestions and encouragement I began revising and expanding the manuscript. I must, therefore, also thank the publishers for their support and expertise in helping turn that manuscript into this book in a few short weeks.

And to think, this little piece of history and the recalling of a formative period of my life almost disappeared without trace.

Neil Murphy

Preface

Five years ago I was walking up Blarney Street in Cork on my first visit for nearly sixty years. For four years during the war I had stayed in my aunt's house on Nicholas Well Lane close to Blarney Street as an evacuee. Now I was back for a nostalgia fest.

Strolling past the dilapidated shops and pubs I suddenly heard in my head a voice saying "Blue Gillette blade, Blue Gillette blade." It happened while passing the pharmacy and that was the instruction from my cousin Billy I would trot down the road repeating.

Triggering like this and the feelings associated with it doesn't always happen, of course, and can't be laid on to order. We are more likely to be taken by surprise by such an instance, experiencing immediate nostalgia, for example, on hearing Vera Lynn singing "there'll be bluebirds over, the White Cliffs of Dover". But while these feelings can induce pleasant memories they can also do the opposite.

For thirty years I was a practicing hypnotherapist. Of almost twenty-five thousand clients over the years, many were experiencing feelings that were having a negative influence on their lives, a negativity, according to Freud, that comes from repressed memories. I can give an example of something in my own life that was a mystery for decades. Although not lacking in self-confidence, every time I approached or was approached by a figure of authority, my left cheek would hurt and glow red. I put myself into a hypnotic trance over this problem and quickly discovered the reason. I was transported back to 1945 to the geography room in De La Salle College in Sheffield. I must have been out of order because our teacher, Brother John, raised his cane and to the horror of the rest of the class, swiped it across my face. This traumatic experience was then buried in my unconscious mind and eventually cause the inappropriate response.

Not long after this bout of self-hypnosis, I attended a fiftieth anniversary reunion of my starting at De La Salle. A schoolmate reminded me of the incident saying he still had nightmares about it. I no longer had the problem. The incident had come to light, taken wings and would never return.

Unfortunately, such things are not always so easily dealt with. Sometimes the hidden memories are so painful clients are unable to face them and unconsciously refuse to let them out. Hypnotherapy, particularly regression, can help but it must be carried out with the utmost care.

One of the things I wanted to do on retirement was use my professional experience to access the period of my childhood in Ireland during World War II. My memories of this eventful time were patchy and sometimes disturbing. I had frequently enabled clients to access their past. Could I now perform the same service on myself?

My method was to use a voice-activated tape-recorder late at night when there was no risk of disturbance from family or telephone. I would begin by entering a womb-like environment of warmth, softness and darkness created with a couple of duvets. It worked beautifully. It would take me a few minutes to enter deep trance and as I began talking, my recorder would switch on. The starting point for my 'case', was my sixth birthday, July 15, 1939.

Once the flow started, there was no stopping it and within weeks I had dictated half a million words. Much of it was banal, even incoherent. Listen to some pre-teens talking when they don't know you're ear-wigging and you will know what I mean! The point is, my loquaciousness was neither conscious nor retrospective; I was actually there in the original setting and situation hearing myself and others speaking.

And it wasn't as if I was just looking and listening. I was, as happens in regression analysis, re-living situations, the affective component, as it is called. I was also feeling the associated emotions of sadness, anger, anxiety and happiness. Sometimes I would come round to find my face wet with tears. And as Eire at that time was bilingual and I picked up the language quite quickly as kids do, I frequently mixed Irish with English on the tape.

On the downside of hypnotherapeutic regression my clients would occasionally become locked in to the world they were visiting, unwilling, or unable to come out of trance. The risk, when putting yourself into a deep hypnotherapeutic state is that you might also get locked in with no one to bring you out of it.

This did happen to me and frightening it was. In the Cork department store fire, for example, I got so upset I was still at the scene after waking in the middle of the night. Even when the 'film spool' ran out, so to speak, I continued to endure serious anxiety. It was one of the most upsetting experiences I have ever had. Most people will have had an intense dream carry on after waking. It is unpleasant but is usually past in a minute. My nightmare, I shall call it, continued for perhaps an hour.

On another of these occasions I became so desperate I dragged myself out of bed and into the garden. Here in the early hours I stripped off and lowered myself into our fish pond. The cold water shocked me back into reality. It gave me confidence to allow myself to go ever deeper into the regression analysis with some startling results. Events, conversations and descriptions of scenes from those war years poured out to be captured on tape.

Once the project was completed I had the tapes typed up and on receipt of the thousand or so pages, got to work with a blue pen. Two thirds of it were cut. "Neil's War" was edited from the remainder.

Being wrenched away from my Mum and home in Sheffield in the North of England almost overnight at the age of six was, I now realized, a traumatic experience. I had suffered separation anxiety, rejection, loneliness and anger at being treated thus. At one point on the tape my Aunt's neighbour rushed in to say Sheffield had been blitzed. My response shocked me. "Good. I hope my bloody Mum and Dad have been killed."

But I was lucky during those four years I didn't get depressed. It certainly developed my confidence (which frequently got me into trouble). I developed an asthma that was almost certainly psychosomatic but I got on with life and overall, remained cheerful. Michael, my elder brother also evacuated, did not respond so well to our new environment and bombs or no he returned to England. My sister Jean coped well, like me. She also became full of herself and remained so until her death half a century later. The reason I kept my head above water was undoubtedly the Irish people. They were unfailingly kind and supportive and I have always felt it was I who let them down.

When I flew back into Dublin in 1953 a few weeks after a ten-year ban on returning had ended, it was typical that those who knew me didn't drag up the past. Those who never knew what had happened during my evacuation years never found out. My Aunt Mary and the rest of the O'Reilly family had kept my secrets safe, as had the government of the day, as governments do. For my part in telling this story I have changed the names of relatives and others closely involved at the time. Many are still alive and I would not want to hurt or upset anyone again.

Here now is my story, "Neil's War".

Chapter One

It's the gas masks that stick in my mind. They smelt horrible when they were strapped to your face. Made you want to be sick. Warm, floppy rubber. I'd had an operation for adenoids two years before and the doctor had stuck a gauze mask over my face and poured some chemical-smelling stuff over it until I fell asleep. I had been frightened and they held me down. And now, as the man in the blue uniform held the gas mask over my face and was playing around with the straps, I had the same feelings. So I gave him a kick. He jumped back and swore at me and Mum was so busy apologizing to him she wasn't bothered about how I felt.

We were in the Edmund Road Drill Hall. A large dirty-looking building that smelt of sweat, leather, cardboard and damp. The windows, those which were not broken, were covered in soot and the only outside you could see was just grey. We'd gone down after tea because everyone had to go. Mum said it was because there might be air raids. And that there could be bombs. And that some of the bombs could be filled with gas. So the Prime Minister said we had to be ready just in case. But Mum didn't think it would happen. We'd only gone because you would be fined if you didn't. So I wasn't bothered.

When we got there it was filled with other people. The men hadn't come because they had got their gas masks at work. So there were a lot of kids screaming. And there were a lot of women huddled into groups and gossiping and shouting at their screaming kids They weren't our type of people. Many of them wore headscarves and raggedy-looking coats and many of their kids had no shoes and snotty noses.

Maureen, our nursemaid who was holding my younger brother Paddy in her arms, slapped me on the ear. "Say sorry to that man. He was only trying to 'elp you. Stop you chokin'. Go on."

"Yes," Mum said in that funny type of voice that she used on the 'phone before she knew who she was talking to. Fishing around in her purse she took out a coin and handed it to the warden.

"He's a naughty boy, Mister Warden. Have a pint of beer on me. He's sorry."

"He don't look that way to me." The warden, pocketing the offering, examined me with a frown. "Not sorry at all. And I've got me job to do you know."

"Just talk to him," Mum encouraged. "Get him to understand."

Going down on one knee he waved the mask in front of me. "Stop your lungs bursting. 'orrible. Drowned in blood. Choke to death."

Mum winced. "Oh ... I don't ..."

"Look, Missus Murphy," my tormentor swung round, "they're watching you know. All these people here. They know Doctor Murphy's lad. Expect better of 'im. Yes, they're watching. Make my job a lot easier if 'e can behive 'imself. So let's get on with it before they all bugger off home."

Maureen, aware that our status on the road was under threat, grabbed my hair and pulling my head back thrust her little brown bottle of smelling salts under my nose. "Sniff that. Go on, take a deep breath then. That's what gas will do to yer. Like it then?" she asked as I squirmed yelling, as the biting fumes shot up my nose.

"It'll be worse than that with 'itlers gas. 'Ave you screaming your 'ed off, pukin' blood."

"It will." The Warden seized eagerly on her contribution. " Lungs bursting. 'orrible ..."

Mum gave a little sob and patted my shoulder. "Do what the man says. Please."

Mum was always using 'please' to get me to do things. But since Paddy had arrived I'd enjoyed ignoring her. I hated Paddy and hated her for having him, so I didn't want to stop being awkward.

Grabbing my arm, Maureen swung me round and waved the little brown bottle. "Want some more of this?" She took the stopper out and waved it over my face.

"That's horrible. Stop being horrible. It burns my nose." I tried to wriggle free but it was no good. Maureen's eyes glared into mine. I knew when she looked at me like that it was no good fighting.

"Can I have some money for sweets, Mum?" The battle was lost but I was determined to retreat with honour.

"Threepence."

"All right then." I turned to the warden and lifted my head. Without another word he deftly slipped the mask over my face and snapped the straps over the back of my head. Grasping the black tin sticking out from the front, the 'pig snout' they called it, he wiggled everything in place and surveyed his handiwork. "See, that doesn't hurt, does it?"

Then the eye holes misted over and everything went dim. Grabbing the straps I pulled the thing off. "I can't see!"

"Oh my God! This is a finicky one, 'ain't 'e just?" He looked at Mum and received another pint of beer. A handkerchief was wiped over the condensation and the mask replaced. This time it wasn't so bad. In fact it felt good. And now I had threepence.

My Dad was a doctor and his practice was in the middle of one of Sheffield's slums. It wasn't a very nice place and it was near Bramall Lane where Sheffield United played. Every Saturday there was roaring from the spectators, like waves coming over our house. This made Dad fed up because he liked to have his forty winks, as he called it, after his dinner before he went off to Wortley Golf Club.

We never played with the kids on the streets around our house. Mum came from the other side of Sheffield. Her father was a forge manager and he was rich. So she didn't think the kids around us were suitable to play with. We used to play with the Cockayne children; they had a large store in the middle of Sheffield, or with other kids who were the children of doctors, most of whom had come across from Ireland with Dad. We were "Doctor Murphy's children" and when we went onto the street at all, which was not very often, as we had a car, the other kids would stop playing and just look at us. I knew that they knew that we were better than them. So we ignored them. Once a little kid came up our drive with an ice-cream and offered me a lick. No one was looking so I took the cone off him and stuck it in his face. Afterwards I felt sorry for what I'd done. But I never told anyone.

"See!" The Warden spun me round, addressing the crowd. "This lad's done it. Doctor Murphy's son. Now you just get on with it too." He signalled the other wardens who had come out of the room at the back with boxes of masks to start handing them round.

Paddy of course, couldn't have a mask as his face was too small. I felt glad as it meant he would choke while we all looked at him from inside our masks. But that wasn't going to happen. Opening a large cardboard box the warden pulled out a Mickey Mouse protector. A large, floppy, black rubber bag to which large black ears and a red nose had been stuck on. Mum, now feeling more confident in her role as Dr. Murphy's wife, walked into the middle of the floor and handed a bewildered-looking Paddy to the head warden who, smart as they come, unzipped the bag, lowered Paddy into its gloomy interior, zipped it up again and invited everyone present to gape at his puce face staring through the stitched-on celluloid screen.

Then, he started pumping a metal handle that ran

to a tube that seemed to enter Mickey Mouse through his bottom. In an instant the bag swelled like a balloon. For a moment I thought he was going to float away up to the ceiling. A thought I think Mum shared, as she started looking worried again.

"Is he alright?" Mum clutched at Maureen,

"Right as ninepence, Missus Murphy."

Bending over a very bloated Mickey, the Warden addressed his audience. "See, this kid is alright. 'E's in the belly of a whale." He looked round to see what impact his well-practised joke had. But I don't think many of them were Bible readers. Staring round at the blank faces, he shrugged and unzipped the bag. A gust of air rushed out and Paddy was returned into the arms of Maureen.

"Would you believe it, Missus Murphy," Maureen examined her charge minutely. "'E's all right. I think 'e enjoyed it!"

Next, Mum, Maureen, my brother Michael and sister Jean were quickly attended to as the assembly murmured appreciatively and then we were done.

"My husband, of course, is too busy to come here."

"Oh yes. We understand, Missus Murphy. We will visit him at the surgery. We must look after our doctor mustn't we!" He gave Mum a tight smile. "Need him around to look after us lot." His hand swept over the throng. "Never fear. We will be up to fit him tomorrow."

Each mask came in a cardboard box with a cord attached, so slinging them over our shoulder, we left the hall in triumph. Hitler could do his worst and we were ready for him. But after a few days the boxes lost their novelty. They were uncomfortable to carry and if you fought with them they split and the mask would drop onto the road. Then they became common. Everyone had one. So the best people bought bright canvas holders that you could slip your box into. Mum thought they were a good idea because they would let people know we were different from the rest of them.

But then we got bored of showing how different we were. When the four of us went for a walk a few days later, we left them behind.

As we were walking down Charlotte Road a policeman with a big moustache came across the road and put his hand up. "And where's your gas masks?"

"Gas masks?" Maureen gaped. "The er ... war hasn't started, has it?"

The policeman stood back. "Not started?" He looked up to the sky and then back at us. "Do you think that Mister 'itler is going to send you a letter saying 'ees on 'is way and that you'd better go 'ome and get your gas masks? Do you?"

"Well ..." Maureen's bravado dissolved. "I didn't think ..."

"Didn't think?" Incredulity strengthened and heightened his voice. "Didn't think?" He looked round at the urchins who had gathered. "Bodies. Little bodies. All over the street. Sick and choking with gas and you didn't think?" He affected a very deep breath. Rolled his eyes. Everyone was looking at him wide-mouthed.

"Get home. Get home now. And don't let me ever see you out here without your gas masks." We stood rigid with fear as he took out a little book and wrote our names down, starting with Maureen's.

"You should have had more sense, Miss. Looking after these little ones!" Shaking his head he slipped his book into his breast pocket and sauntered off.

Fumbling in her bag, Maureen took out her smelling salts and inhaled so deeply her head shot back and her eyes watered. Wiping her eyes she glared after the departing figure. "Oos 'e think 'e is," she addressed the gathering. Swinging the pram round she marched off. "I'll show 'im, I will."

But she never showed anyone. By the time we reached home, her fury had abated and raising the matter with Mum would only mean another application of smelling salts and more tears so she just left us in the nursery and retired to her bedroom.

Then there was the sirens. Everyone had been warned about them. The Evening Star was enjoying itself. Big, black headlines blared out from the news stands. It would happen at six o'clock, just as the news came on the Home Service. We weren't to worry. It was a practice. Just a pretend. But pretend or not it was frightening. I'd once watched a dog die at the bottom of our drive. A van had hit it and crushed its back end. For hours it lay there making a horrible whining noise until a policeman came along and shot it. The sirens reminded me of that dog, only the whining noise was stronger. And it seemed to get inside me. As if that dog was in my tummy. I could feel my tummy trembling. So could

Jean but she started to cry. I didn't. Then Jean wet herself and Maureen had to fetch dry knickers for her. And by the time she'd done that the sirens had stopped.

I didn't sleep very well that night. I was all tense waiting for the sirens. And when it happened again a few days later I was so frightened I jumped out of bed and raced across the landing to Mum's room. But I went so fast I couldn't stop at her door and instead went straight down the stairs and lay like a hedgehog moaning on the hall floor. No bones were broken, however, so Dad lifted me back to bed and just as he tucked me in, the 'all clear' went. They were going to Manchester he reassured me.

After that, 'going to Manchester' became the stock phrase. Dad took out an atlas and drew a line that went from Germany to Manchester and showed me how the line crossed Sheffield. Manchester seemed a very bad place to live.

Uncle Bill visited us at the end of August, before war had broken out. He just turned up at our front door all posh-looking in his RAF officer's uniform. He was a trained pilot, the wings on his chest confirmed this, but he had moved to the Volunteer Reserve so that he could go and work in Canada as an engineer and come back if war started. He was back, ready. He brought the three of us moccasin sandals covered in lots of little coloured beads. He said the Indians had made them. Mum was happy to see him. They were very close and when she realised he was going to war she started crying. He didn't seem to mind though. I think he was looking forward to it. He was very handsome, tall with dark wavy hair and a kind smile. Maureen got all funny when he was around and kept finding reasons to come into the lounge to ask silly questions. Mum said she was a flighty bit and needed watching.

A few weeks earlier Dad had swept into the garage late one night and in his headlights seen Maureen being pushed against the back wall by a Guardsman in a red tunic with black trousers. He had come from Glossop Road barracks but, when Dad saw him, his trousers were down. Nobody told me about it. The shouting and screaming woke me up and I looked out of my bedroom window. The car lights were still on and I could see the Guardsman being chased out of our backyard by Dad hitting him on the head. Maureen was crying and Mum was in her dressing gown shouting at her.

The following morning Mum told me she had gone home to see her mother but when she came back a few days later nobody said anything about what had happened. I asked Mum about it and she told me that Maureen had been taken sick and the soldier had tried to help her. She never explained why he had his trousers off and when I asked, Jean glared at me, so I shut up.

A few days later, when I got up for a wee during the night I heard some whispering in Maureen's room and as I stopped to listen, Uncle Bill came out in his pyjamas. As his trousers weren't off I knew Maureen wasn't sick and that made me feel happy. Seeing me on the landing he whispered he had gone to see Maureen to get a glass of water, so I went back to bed. The funny thing was he didn't have a glass in his hand. The next morning I told Mum she should put a glass and some water in Uncle Bill's bedroom but she just looked at me funny and sent me out to play.

The following Sunday we went with Maureen to see her mother. Mrs. Wilson was an old lady of about fifty and she lived in a little back-to-back house in Heeley. There was only one room downstairs and a little kitchen at the back. Mrs. Wilson worked in a sweet factory so she always had lots of liquorish allsorts and Jean used to sit eating them until her face was all smeared in black. Mr. Wilson was dead but he had a hut in the garden which he had fitted out with a model railway which ran on tracks around the wall. Michael and I were allowed to go to the hut while Maureen and her mother talked and Jean stuffed herself with sweets.

Usually we went to see Mrs. Wilson on Saturdays but as we went along Bramall Lane we would meet crowds of men going to the United ground and some of them would talk to Maureen and sometimes they would talk a lot and this would make us late. So I told Mum and she said we could go on Sundays instead. Maureen didn't like that and called me a little snitch, but that didn't change things.

On the first Sunday of the new arrangement we set off after coming home from early Mass. Mum seemed to be worrying and was snapping at everyone. Dad said he wasn't going golfing and he stayed in the lounge listening to the wireless. It was a long way to Mrs. Wilson's house but as the weather was nice, we didn't mind. Maureen said how quiet it was and then suddenly it wasn't quiet any more. There was a car engine roaring and a squeaking of brakes and Mum pulled up to the pavement.

"Quickly!" She seemed terrified. "War's started. Get in the car ..." Jumping out she unstrapped Paddy from his pram, pushed him into Jean's arms and herded us onto the back seat.

"What about the pram, Missus Murphy?"

"Oh ... you'll have to bring it home." Then she revved the engine, swung round and left Maureen standing on the pavement.

Jean started whining. "What about Maureen. Will the Germans bomb her?"

"Goodness, no. It's Sunday."

"But ..."

"They don't bomb people on a Sunday." Mum was getting exasperated. "It would be a mortal sin."

"Well," Jean persisted, "bombing people is a mortal sin, so can it be a worse mortal sin on a Sunday?"

"Shut up!" Mum said. She slowed down as a policeman in a black helmet stepped off the pavement and waved her down.

"War's started missus. Where are you going?"

"I'm taking the children to their uncle's house at Sandygate."

The policeman's eyes searched around the car's interior. "With no gas masks?" He pulled his notebook from his pocket. "It's an offence you know. And what about these kids. Yours, are they?"

"They had their gas masks." Mum was almost weeping. "I left them in the pram."

"I don't see no pram, missus."

"I've left it with their nanny."

"Nanny?" He raised his eyebrows. "And where is this lady?"

"Mummy just dumped her," Jean said, "left her to be bombed."

He looked at Mum thoughtfully. "Where?"

"Back there."

"Heeley?"

"By the bridge. All on her own," Jean added.

"She's not far from her mother's," Mum said in defence. "She can go there. I was going to pick her up later."

"And leave your kids without their gas masks?"

"All right." Mum ground the gears and her teeth. "I'll go back now."

"I think you should. At once." Tipping his helmet the policeman walked into the middle of the road and signalled whatever traffic there was to stop while Mum swung round.

Maureen had reached her mum's by the time we got to Heeley. As we walked in, Jean said we were sorry for leaving her. Mum said there was no need to apologise. Mrs. Wilson said that there certainly was. Maureen said they were looking for girls for the munitions factory and that she would be going there where she would get some respect. Mrs. Wilson said her son would wheel the pram back when he got back from fishing but it would cost half a crown and that he would bring Maureen's case back with him.

25

Mum paid over the money. Michael piled the gas masks into the car. Jean kissed Maureen, who had tears her eyes and said goodbye. I said goodbye but didn't kiss her. Mum said nothing. And off we went.

The next time I saw Maureen the war was over. She was married to the owner of the factory where she had been working. She was very rich and had a big house and two sons and she was very nice to us. Maureen cried when I told her about Uncle Bill being killed and stroked the hair of her oldest son who was called William. I told her I liked reading the 'William' stories. Jean said that William was Uncle Bill's name. Maureen gave her a very long look. Then Jean cried because she was Jean. And I ate a big bag of sweets which her mother had brought home from work.

Michael, Jean and I stayed at Uncle David's that night. Uncle David had two steel works and was rich. His wife had a sewing machine company and she was rich. They had no children and when we visited they always looked at us funnily as if we were going to blow up. They lived in a big house on the edge of the moors and however rich they were the Germans wouldn't bother to fly over to Sandygate to bomb one house so Mum said we would be safe there.

The floors of Gartmore, which was what it was called, were all polished. No carpets at all. It was a gloomy place and seemed like a church. Auntie Grace was waiting for us in the porch when we arrived. She had a smile on as if she didn't mean it. Uncle David was very hearty but I don't think he meant it either.

After putting our stuff into our bedrooms we went down to tea. Jean was unhappy because she wanted to sleep with us but Auntie Grace said little girls didn't sleep in boys' rooms. Jean said she did at home and she wasn't little, she was grown-up. And why shouldn't grown-up girls sleep in boys' rooms? Auntie Grace's lips started to look tight and her voice became like my teacher's when anyone couldn't tell her how to spell beautiful.

"Because ..." she started and then stopped to take us down to the dining room where the table was piled up with plates of bread and honey and lemonade. I cleared my plate in less than five minutes and as Jean wasn't eating much, I leaned over and took some of hers too. We'd never had honey at home so I didn't know I had an allergy to the stuff. Just as I was finishing I felt a queasiness running from my tummy to my throat and then, before I could do anything about it, a gush of sick shot out of my mouth all over the table.

For a moment there was silence as I looked at the creamy fluid floating in little islands over the table, on the glasses of lemonade and on the floor. Jean, always very proper, let out a scream and jumping off her chair stood crying. Michael, overcome with laughing, fell off his chair and rolled around on the floor. Then Jean cried even more and ran out of the room and up the stairs shouting "I hate you. You're horrible."

Uncle David and Auntie Grace said nothing but just sat there looking as if they'd been hit on the head with a cricket bat.

We were too far away from Sheffield to hear the sirens but Mum, in the centre of things, rang up in the middle of the night to tell Uncle David they had gone off. He dragged us out of bed and down the stairs and bundled us under the arch of the staircase. Auntie Grace brought some rugs and we sat there 'til daylight as Mum had forgotten to ring and say the 'all clear' had gone off.

After breakfast she turned up at Gartmore to take us for a walk to the Botanical Gardens. She gave us some money for ice-cream, dropped us at the entrance and tootled off. She was always 'tootling off' to do things which meant Cole Brothers where she would sit having coffee with friends. But this time, she told us, she was making arrangements. We were going to stay with Dad's family in Ireland to get away from the bombs. She didn't know how long we would be away but she would be happy knowing we were safe. Jean and I thought this sounded great. Michael, being the eldest, was less happy and told Mum she was just getting rid of us.

As we walked round the gardens, Jean was sad, Michael was angry and I looked at the squirrels. I wanted to be off and was already a bit fed up waiting around. Jean then went off into fairy land as usual and Michael forgot about the ice-creams and when Mum came back he also forgot to give her the money back.

Chapter Two

Sheffield station, the LMS one, was full of people when we arrived. It was only six o'clock and it was cold and the smoke and steam from the engines was crawling over the platforms as it couldn't get away because of the glass roof. Buses were arriving with kids and their brown paper parcels. A lot of children had no suitcases because they never went on holiday. But we had leather ones. Mum had bought them specially and they looked very smart.

There were also groups of kids in school uniforms. One large group near us were in Notre Dame blazers and Dad, as we were Catholics, went and talked to one of the teachers. She said they had rented an old hall in Derbyshire and they were going to stay there for the duration. I didn't understand what the word meant but Dad said it meant "as long as the war lasted."

Mum said she wouldn't want to go where they were going because the old hall, which was called Derwent Hall, was just in front of the big dam. If the Germans bombed the wall down they would be washed away. She told us that where we were going was much safer as the Irish weren't at war with Germany.

There were a lot of crying babies and a lot of cry babies who were hanging on to their mothers' hands as if they didn't want to go. Maybe if they cried hard enough they'd all go back home and forget about going away.

But I wanted to go. At least I was sure I did. The only thing was that Mum didn't know when we could be coming back. She said "maybe Christmas." But I don't think she really knew and only said it to keep Michael quiet.

I killed thirty Germans on the way to Liverpool. Dad said they were just sheep but I knew that they were soldiers pretending to be sheep. Jean said I was stupid and wanted me to stop as there was a lot of smoke coming in through the window and the ashes were getting in her eyes and anyway the bangs from my cap pistol were giving her a headache. Michael stayed quiet. He had been crying when we left Mum at the station and after a lot of nose-blowing he was pretending to read his comic but he wasn't really.

Before we got to Liverpool where the ship was, we had to go through Manchester and I didn't want to go to Manchester as I knew the Germans were always coming to bomb it. Dad said there was nothing we could do as the track went through Manchester and that maybe I should sit still as they wouldn't be coming until midnight and by that time we would be in Liverpool.

It got darker and darker as we went across the moors and everything looked very lonely. After a while, when it was very dark a little blue light came on. Dad said all the bulbs had been taken out so the bombers couldn't see us. I thought that was a good idea. But not too good as I couldn't read my comic and Micheal had to stop pretending he was reading his comic. So he just sat sniffing and I kept snapping my gun. I had run out of caps so I was getting bored.

Just as we were coming into Manchester I cocked my gun again and got ready for if any bombers came. But they didn't so I started rubbing my lip with my gun. Then the hammer snapped and caught my lip and I screamed. Dad asked what was wrong. He couldn't see me in the dim light. Then I started crying as it was hurting more. I pulled at the gun and turned it over but that only made it worse as it pulled my lip deep inside where all the works were. I could feel the slippery blood on my hands. Even though he was a doctor, Dad didn't know what to do as he couldn't see me and was worried that he might make things worse. A man sitting beside me said he would go and ask the guard to put the light back on.

When the guard came he lit a match and said "Oh, my God!" But he wouldn't put the light on as the bombers coming to Manchester might see the light and bomb us. Dad pushed his hanky into my hand and told me to use it to soak up the blood. He said we would be in Manchester soon and the station would be lit up then he could sort it out. But he was wrong. The station was so dark we didn't know we were there until the train stopped.

Finally, Dad got out and called for the guard. He had a big lamp that shone red and green. Dad asked him to shine the red on my face and then played around with the gun. Then the guard brought a little screwdriver and turned a screw on the handle and the gun went into two pieces and fell off. Then I fainted.

I was always fainting. It never bothered me. I used to do it at Mass when the priest got boring. I used to fall onto the floor and Dad used to have to carry me out. I used to faint at school as well but *Mademoiselle* got used to it and would just lay me on the floor. Dad said it was because I had low blood pressure. Jean used to hate it when I fainted because she thought I was going to die. But I couldn't help it.

The train guard was upset that I had delayed the train. They wanted to take me to hospital. Dad said no. He was a doctor and that I would be all right. I wanted the train to go on because I thought I could hear the bombers coming. The guard said they weren't because we would have heard the sirens. Then he got out of the carriage and blew his whistle and waved his lamp and the train moved off. Jean said she hated me as I could have had them all killed because of my silly gun. Then, as we left the station, the sirens went off and the driver speeded the train up and we went on to Liverpool.

The train didn't stop at Liverpool. It rushed straight through to the docks. Dad said it was a boat train for people going to Ireland and if people in Liverpool wanted to go on it they would catch a tram to the docks.

The train stopped when it reached the docks. Dad said it was a wide river, the Mersey. As it stopped a man came along and told us not to get out. We would have to wait. So I sat and looked at the Mersey.

The moon was very bright and you could see everything very clearly. Dad said that was bad because if the bombers came they could see everything too. There were a lot of ships floating on the Mersey. I counted thirty-four then I stopped counting because it made my eyes tired. Dad said they were nearly all navy ships and he pointed out a cruiser and far away, the big black shape of an aircraft carrier. Nearest was a destroyer but everyone seemed to be asleep on it because it had no lights. Dad said that was because they didn't want the submarines to see them. He said there were a lot of submarines around and that they poked up out of the water and fired torpedoes to blow ships up. This made me feel happy I wasn't on the water until I remembered that was what we were soon going to do.

There were balloons over most of the ships. The moonlight made them look silver. You could just make out the cables holding them down as the moon reflected off them. The balloons were swaying a little. It looked as if they were asleep as well. Dad said they were about two thousand feet high and were there waiting for a bomber to hit them. That seemed stupid to me because if I could see the ballons the bombers could too and they could swing away from them.

Dad said maybe.

For a long time nothing happened. Dad said they

were waiting for our ship to come from Ireland and after everyone had got off we could get on. He didn't know how long that would take. Dad lifted me up onto the luggage rack and told me to go to sleep. Just as I was doing that the sirens went and I jumped down again. After a few minutes some of the ships started firing their guns. Dad said I was to get on the floor. Jean got down so far that she got under the seat. Michael didn't seem to be bothered and opened the carriage window and leaned out. Dad said he was to come back in as there could be *shrapnel* from the guns, but he didn't. He just put his comic over his head.

As I leaned out beside him the firing got worse and then suddenly an aeroplane with two engines came roaring along the river. It had no lights on but I could see the flames from its exhaust. As it ran over the ships there was more shooting. Then it disappeared and the shooting stopped. Dad said it had gone out to sea but it had to come back as it had to go along the river to get home. He was right. After a minute or two I could hear it again. This time none of the ships shot at it but as it went over one ship, Dad said it was the aircraft carrier, a searchlight switched on and turned on the plane. That was clever because it seemed to have blinded the pilot so he couldn't see where he was going.

The plane swung to the right and left to get away from the beam but it was no good. Just as it passed our train one of its wings hit one of the balloon cables. The cable hung onto the wing and the plane went round in a circle. Then the wing broke off and the plane fell into the Mersey. A fountain of water went high into the air and it was like a firework as the moon flashed on the drops. Then ripples swept out to the other side and came back again getting smaller and smaller. A minute later a boat came over to where the plane had sunk. It circled round for a few minutes and then it went back to shore. Then everything went dark again. I climbed back onto the luggage rack. For a while I couldn't go to sleep as I was so excited but then I did.

Sometimes when you are thinking about things that happened you can't remember everything all the time and the next thing I remembered was going up the gangway of the ship. It was called Lady Leinster and it seemed to be a big ship. On its side, just below the gangway, a huge flag had been painted. It was in three colours, green, white and orange. The flag was fresh but everything else looked dirty. There was black paint and rust and some white paint that was flaking and very dirty. It didn't look safe to me but Dad said it was twenty years old and he'd been on it before and I wasn't to worry.

A man was waiting for us at the top of the gangway. He took us through a door and down some steel steps and into a sort of dining room with lots of dirty tables with beer bottles on them and some cups and plates. He seemed nice, he said that he was a steward and asked us what we wanted to eat. He didn't wait for an answer as he said that there was only one choice. It was biscuits and milk or milk and biscuits.

Two moments later he came back with a tray. He

told Jean she was having milk and biscuits but because we were boys we would have to settle for biscuits and milk. Jean and I laughed but Michael didn't. He said he wanted tea. The man pretended to look surprised. I think he was trying to be funny. There was no tea, he said as there was no hot water. If Michael (he called him *Mihaul*, as that was the Irish name for Michael) wanted tea they would have to get some from the engine room and then the ship couldn't sail as it needed hot water to drive the engines. Jean just looked at him in a funny way and said he was being silly. The man then took off his cap and bowed to Jean and called her 'Madam' and said "aren't you a clever one then *Mavourneen*?" Jean giggled at that.

Then he asked us what our cabin number was and Dad came across the dining room and showed him a ticket. I said I didn't want to go to bed because I wanted to go on deck and watch the ships. He became very serious. Going on deck was forbidden, he said. The captain would be cross if he saw us there as it was dangerous for children at night because he wouldn't be able to see if we fell into the sea. We had to remember that or he would be in trouble as it was his job to look after us.

Dad had met some other men and they were playing cards and drinking. He said "night, night" after we had finished our supper and the steward guided us out of the dining room and along a white corridor and opened a door. Our cabin was painted white and it had three bunks. He put our cases down and told us to get to bed as they were ready to sail.

He said his name was Seamus and if we needed something we should press the bell by the door. He was very cheerful and said that he probably wouldn't hear it but it was worth a try. But we would be better off if we just got into our bunks and went to sleep.

After he had gone, Jean said that he was a really silly man. Michael fought me for the top bunk. I got into my pyjamas and took the bottom one. Then the ship started rumbling and I could feel it going up and down.

A big bump woke me up. There was a little blue light on in the cabin and Jean and Michael were asleep. For a while I lay there listening. Then there was another bump, a bit harder this time and the ship wasn't rumbling and I knew the engines had stopped. I went to the porthole to look out but it had been blackouted with thick paint and I couldn't see anything. Opening the door I went slowly into the corridor. There were voices coming from the dining room and I could hear Dad and Seamus talking about their card game. They were taking no notice of anyone so I slipped past, up the steep steps and out onto the deck.

Near the front of the ship there were some men talking. As I moved closer I could see another ship touching ours. That was what must have made the bang. The other ship looked funny at first, like a pepper pot. But as I got closer I saw it was a submarine. My mouth opened. It was just its conning tower and there was a big gun on it. There were some sailors standing there and as I watched, a sailor on our ship threw a rope across to one of the sailors on the tower and he caught it and tied it around something. Next, another man who was wearing a peaked cap pulled himself along the rope and came over the railings of our ship and started talking to our sailors. I think one of them was the captain because he had lots of rings on his sleeve.

I felt a bit frightened as I remembered what Dad had said about submarines blowing up ships but the group of men at the front didn't seem frightened. Someone had brought a bottle along and they were all taking swigs from it.

The man from the submarine was talking about a searchlight and as he did, a sailor leaned over from the bridge of the ship and lowered something on a rope. Dragging it along the deck they pulled out some wires and plugged them in. Suddenly everything became very bright and I was spotted.

"You have a spy!" The submarine man had a long, narrow face and a pointy beard and a happy laugh. "I have just seen him!" Then he came along and picked me up and carried me along to where the submarine was tied on.

"You want to come with me?" There was a lot of laughing as I stood there in my pyjamas feeling rather silly. "Would you like to come to Germany?"

"I'm going to Ireland. With my Dad. He won't let me."

"But you would come?"

"If Michael and Jean could too. Maybe"

"Three of you!" He turned away and watched as the ship's crew wrestled with the big light they were fixing to the rails. "On the port side too!" he shouted.

The captain of the Lady Leinster seemed to be getting impatient. "We'll be missing the tide in Dublin if we hang around much longer, Captain."

Putting me down the submariner waved a finger in front of our captain. "If you don't get those lights going you mightn't get to Dublin at all my friend. Why was your flag not lit up? There are others of my comrades around here. A darkened ship without identification is in danger of being sunk." Then he looked at me.

"Go back to bed, little boy. You will be safe."

"Do you work for Mister Hitler?"

"Ha, ha!" he guffawed. "Mister Hitler? Yes. He is my friend!"

"Well, he doesn't seem to be a nice man ..."

Our ship's captain cut in and hissed "go back to bed. And shut up."

By this time Seamus had come on deck. Sizing up the situation he grabbed my arm. "Come on you. You'll be getting us all wet feet."

As he led me back down he said "there's been a ship sunk just off Galway. The Athenia. There's been over a hundred kids drowned. Count yourself lucky this captain has given us a chance. Ours is in too much of hurry. Should have had our flag lit up."

Opening the cabin door he pushed me in and shut it with a bang.

"What have you been doing?" Jean asked sleepily.

"I've just been to the lavatory." Flopping back into my bunk I pulled the pillow over my head. As soon as I felt the ship pitching again I fell asleep.

Chapter Three

As we steamed into Cork station there was a group of old ladies waiting for us. They all had those silly hats on with birds and feathers and stuff. They were Dad's sisters. They seemed very happy to see him. They didn't take any notice of us.

Dad was a sort of hero. His Dad had run a pig factory which made bacon and pork and sausages and pies. They also made *drisheen*, something so horrible you'd have to be weird to like it as it consisted of dried blood made up into sausage shapes. As we soon found out you had it with milk and pepper and then if you were lucky you didn't puke it all up again.

They were quite well-off and were brought up in a big house called Pouladuff. But Dad was the only one who had gone to university. They'd spent a lot of money for him to go there but when he had finished he went off to England like most of his friends. Everyone seemed to think that was the right thing to do.

One lady came across and looked at us and said, "So this is your brood, Willy?"

Another lady, she seemed really old, said, "You're a fine-looking bunch. But you look thin. We'll fatten you up, God help us!"

There was a lot of "God help us" with the Murphy family and I wondered why they didn't go and help themselves for a change. Looking at them with their fat bums and thick legs I thought God might get around to helping them by letting them starve a bit. They all talked a lot and didn't seem to listen to what anyone else was saying. They reminded me of the starlings on the front lawn at home.

We left the station in a trap. That's a sort of a cart pulled by a horse. There were a lot of them around because they didn't have much petrol due to the war. Ireland, or Eire as they called it, was neutral and the man in charge who was called de Valera, wasn't very friendly to the English because they shot his friends a few years ago during a revolution. But, so my cousin Billy told me later, he had to pretend to be friendly because he was frightened the English would stop sending coal over. Some people say they didn't shoot him because he told the British about his friends and what they were doing. That he was a spy. But others say it was because he was born in America and the English didn't want to upset the Americans. I don't know. And I didn't really care. As long as no-one tried to shoot me.

There were some cars around, with big bags full of gas which people had taken from their cookers, which they used instead of petrol. These bags were tied onto their roofs and had dangly pipes to their engines. They looked as if they were about to fly off. There were lots of people walking about. Most of the women wore black shawls over their heads. And there were a lot of priests in cassocks. People were wheeling barrows full of coal or vegetables. They all looked poor.

But Cork was much nicer than Sheffield. There were lots of bridges and rivers and the sea came right into the place so there were always seagulls flying around and screeching. And the air was lovely and fresh, not like gloomy smelly Sheffield. I decided I was going to like it.

We were staying with Auntie Mary. She seemed a nice person. Her hair was silver with lots of little curls but she seemed sad. Dad told us her son, who was as old as me, had died the year before. He was just found dead in the morning when she went to wake him up. After a while I used to catch her looking at me crying. Clare told me her mother had said Jesus had sent me to replace her Brendan.

Clare thought that was funny because Brendan was a little angel but I was more like a *leprechaun*, whatever that was. Clare was Auntie Mary's daughter. She was in the trap with us. She didn't look sad at all. She was older, I think about ten, but I liked her. She had a lot of ginger hair which was made up in curls. Her face was very pale and she had a lot of freckles. She seemed to think everything that happened was funny. As we went up a steep hill from the station the horse puffed like an old man and then blew a fart.

Clare let out a laugh and Michael and I laughed as well but Auntie Mary just looked a bit funny and didn't say anything apart from "Clare!"

We drove into Nicholas Well Lane. It was a

horrible narrow place and the trap wheels scraped the walls. The driver said, "bejasus Missus O'Reilly we'll be stuck like a cork if we go any further."

Auntie Mary said "you'll be getting no fare from me Liam, if you don't get us to the house. We've all this luggage. We can't carry that."

Eventually we scraped round a corner and in front of us was a large cobbled square. It was a lot like round our house in Sheffield. There were slum houses like on Charlotte Road but they didn't have an upstairs and were more like cottages. But at one side of the square there were two big houses. Well, not big but bigger than the others. Auntie Mary's house was one of them and the other, which stood higher and seemed bigger than hers, was painted in dark red. Auntie Mary's house had a big garden with a wall at the end and a red gate that lead in from the lane.

As we went in, a short fat man was standing at the door. He had a round head which looked as if it was iced with short white hair. His face was flushed and his nose was red as a plum. He was wearing braces into which his thumbs were stuck and he didn't look happy to see us. Auntie Mary said that was Uncle Tom.

I said hello to Uncle Tom and Michael said hello. He looked at us without saying anything at first, then he said "so, you're running away from Mister Hitler!"

For Michael, leaving Sheffield was bad but faced with sneering he lost his temper and put his fists up. "As soon as I'm old enough I'll be going back to fight. So there!" He glared at his uncle. "You're just a silly old fool." Then he burst into tears.

"Leave them alone Tom," Auntie Mary said quietly, "and help us with their bags. But he just stood back from the door and watched Auntie Mary and Dad carry the stuff in. Then as soon as that was done, Dad said he had to go, as Jean was staying at Auntie Bridget's house and he wanted to see her settled in. They had gone off in another trap to a village called Douglas nearby where Auntie Bridget lived. He promised he would come back before he set off back to England but he didn't because I didn't see him again for four years.

As I stood in the hall, Uncle Tom asked me if I had any money. I said I had half a crown. "Shall we change that into five shillings!" he said. Then he picked his hat off a stand and catching my arm took me off down the path with Clare following. Michael didn't come. I think he had already decided he hated Uncle Tom.

Uncle Tom seemed to be happy to be out of the house. I think he was the kind of person a lot of people were rude to, so he was not bothered by Michael not coming. He started singing something like "umpty tiddly eyti oh ..." A song with no real words and Clare started skipping and singing along with him.

At the end of Nicholas Well Lane there were a lot of steps which they called the Rock Steps and when you stood at the top you could see the river and all of the city in front of you. Also at the bottom was the *Gardai* Barracks. In Ireland *Gardai* is what they call the police. And they call a police station a barracks.

As we passed the barracks there was a crowd gathering, a few old women with shawls over their heads who were called shawlies and a group of kids. There was a large black van. Then just as we arrived three men came out of the barracks dressed as airmen with helmets and goggles. They were wet and looked cold. They also looked fed up. Behind them was a *Garda* in his peaked cap. We joined the spectators and Uncle Tom strolled across and patted the *Garda* on his shoulder.

"Where are these fellers from Colum? They look perished."

The officer looked round carefully. "They've just been picked up in a dinghy at Crosshaven. Came down in the sea. Lost their way. Ran out of fuel. The lifeboat's brought them up the river."

"Taking them to prison camp are ye?"

"Ah, no Tom. We've had orders to send the poor lads home. There's a ship at Pope's Quay going to Cardiff. We're putting them on it."

"Whose decision is that, then?"

The *Garda* lowered his voice. "The big man's. Dev's. He just wants them out of the way."

"And what if the Germans hear you're letting them go?"

The *Garda* shrugged. "They won't, unless you pass on the news. And you won't be doing that will you, Tom O'Reilly?" He raised his eyebrows for a moment then he turned away and shepherded the airmen into the van which had backed up.

They looked very tired and I felt sorry for them.

I had read a lot of Biggles books and felt I knew how they were feeling. I took out my half-crown to pass it to them so they could buy something but Uncle Tom grabbed my hand. "Sure they'll be looked after like princes when they get on the boat. Keep your money for yourself." To demonstrate his good intentions he shouted across, "best of luck, lads!"

One of them waved over his shoulder. But none of them looked back.

Then Uncle Tom turned to us. "Come on, we're off to town. Over the bridge we go."

Hurrying over North Gate Bridge we went up North Main Street and into St. Patrick's Street which is the town centre.

"Slow down, Daddy," Clare called. "For God's sake me legs are falling off. They won't have run out of beer by the time you get there!"

John Rings was a small pub in an alleyway just off St. Patrick's Street. Uncle Tom pushed us in and we crowded onto a bench. Nobody seemed to notice us and nobody seemed bothered we were children. The place felt really nice. People were playing cards. There was cigarette ash on the tables and on the floor. Ashtrays were filled with butt ends, some of them still smouldering. There were glasses everywhere and lots and lots of talking and laughing.

As Uncle Tom went off to the bar I smiled at Clare. A lot of people knew her and talked to her and her eyes shone. She was enjoying herself. But I felt a bit nervous as it was all strange but I found that talking to Clare made me feel better.

"So how long have I got to put up with you in my house?" she said, just as I was thinking this.

"I don't know. Maybe Christmas."

She rolled her eyes. "As long as that?"

I shrugged. "There's no need to be horrible. What can I do?"

"You can behave yourself and do what I say for a start."

"But ..."

"There'll be no 'buts'," she cut in sharply. "You're like beggars. You don't argue."

Uncle Tom came back with a tray of drinks and frowned. "What's up with you? You look as if you've lost a pound and found a penny."

"It's her." I was a tiny bit tearful. "She says we're not wanted. We're beggars."

"Ah now, she's only pulling your leg." He put his hand out. "I'll have that half-crown now. Take no notice of Clare. She's only trying to get a rise out of you."

Sitting down he tipped his head back and I watched his Guinness draining. When the glass was half empty he wiped his lips. "Can you sing, Niall?"

"My name's Neil, not Niall."

"You'll be Niall in Ireland. That's what everyone will call you, lad." He wiped his lips again. "You'd best get used to it and fit in. All round here was burnt to ashes by Englishmen, Black and Tans. People have long memories. Cork people have long memories. So don't get on any high horse. Then you'll be alright."

He became absorbed by his Guinness again,

drinking it and looking at it. Then he lit a fag and turned back to me. "Do you sing, lad, I asked?"

"Like a frog, I guess!" Clare sniggered.

I gave her a black look. "I can. I'm very good. But only in the choir at church. I can't sing on my own. I'm shy."

"Is that true?"

I started singing 'I'll sing a hymn to Mary', not loud just quietly. That was my favourite at St. Mary's and people used to say how lovely it sounded.

"For God's sake, Niall!" Clare snorted. "Can't you do better than that?" She wrinkled her nose. "Hymns for God's sake. Don't you know 'The Harp that Once'?"

"I know 'O Danny Boy'." I knew that one because Dad had a record of it. He used to play it in the evening and I would sing along with it. That would make him a bit teary when I did. I think it made him sad.

"Danny Boy would be lovely. Go on then," Uncle Tom encouraged.

So, taking a deep breath I started. My teacher said my voice was pure as a bell. It reminded her of an angel. I used to feel really good when I was singing. When you can hear yourself doing something good you feel so much better and your singing gets better. By the time I'd reached 'the pipes, the pipes are calling', the pub was quiet and everyone was turning and looking at me. Even the man behind the bar stopped pumping beer.

Even though I blushed, I enjoyed myself because I'm a bit of a show-off and it was one in the eye for

Clare to give her something to think about. Beggars don't sing like angels!

Everyone stayed quiet until I finished the verse and then they clapped.

"He's from England and he's been bombed by those Germans." Uncle Tom stood up and blew his nose with a large handkerchief. "We've taken him in, God help us! His brother as well. His mother ..." Then he acts choked up and tears run down his cheeks. "His poor mother, God rest her soul ..."

Clare gave me a nudge. "Take no notice. He's just telling a tale. He gets more money if he can get them to cry! Can't you try to look sad?" Since I had seen Mum only yesterday I knew she was alright so I wasn't bothered.

Coming around the table, Uncle Tom put his hanky in his pocket and his upturned hat on the table and wrapped his arm around my shoulder.

"God help us! Sure the poor lad misses his mammy. And if you would like to give a little 'thank you' for that lovely singing I'm sure it would be appreciated." Then he went off to the toilet leaving me feeling like a fool.

The chinking had fallen to a dribble when he came back. He picked his hat up, tumbled the offerings into his pocket and nodded to Clare. "We'll be taking him to Saint Augustine's now," he addressed his audience again. He has some prayers to say and wants to light a candle."

"Jesus, that was great Daddy." Clare's eyes were bright as we scooted down the alley. "Didn't you think so Niall?"

I didn't know what to think. I didn't feel upset because I knew he was telling lies. At any rate I thought I would go along with it. If Clare thought it was great, I did too. She terrified me because she was so sure of herself. I wasn't going to get on the wrong side of her.

We went down another narrow street. Uncle Tom pulled a bunch of keys out and opened the door of a large, dirty-looking shop which had the words O'Reilly, Plumbers over the entrance.

"This is Daddy's shop," Clare said, sweeping her arm round. "Isn't it great?"

But it wasn't great. Apart from a counter on which Uncle Tom tumbled the money from his pocket, there was nothing but empty shelves. There was some pipe and a couple of taps but nothing else apart from an old sink and other rubbish lying in the corner.

"Four pounds, ten shillings and ninepence. Now isn't that great!" He looked at me. "We'll be partners, Clare and you and me."

"That'll be great!" Clare said. Everything to those two was great. But I felt it would be greater still if he gave me my half-crown back.

He shoveled the money back into his pocket. "We'll go to Blarney tomorrow. Get him on top of the place. That'll be great, won't it?"

"What for, Daddy?"

"He's too shy. But a great voice. The two of ye will be doing great things once we've dealt with that."

"Great things for who, Daddy?" Clare winked.

God, she had a lovely smile. It made me feel as if I wanted to go to the toilet.

Auntie Mary didn't look very pleased when we got back. She had made a big meal and, apart from what Michael had eaten, the stuff was looking a bit cold and forlorn.

"Be careful of trips out with your Uncle Tom." She waggled her finger at me. "He'll get you up to a lot of no good. What have you been doing?"

"Nothing Mammy." Clare winked at me. "Just showing Niall the sights."

Next Sunday, after Mass, we set off for Blarney Castle. Up Blarney Street, along Sunday's Well and out into the country. Uncle Tom didn't make Mass, as he had 'other business'. As we passed the asylum, just getting into the open country, the little Austin started weaving across the road, swerved to avoid a lorry and ended up in a ditch. Getting out Uncle Tom staggered onto the road then fell flat on his face.

"So now we know what his 'other business' was," said Auntie grimly. She climbed out of the car and belaboured her husband with her umbrella. "Get up you drunken eejit. Jesus, Mary and Joseph it's a wonder you didn't have us all killed."

She stood looking at him but all he could do was moan.

"Right, then, we'll leave you to it, Tom O'Reilly." Climbing in behind the wheel she drove off, leaving Uncle Tom sitting in the grass scratching his head.

We went to the Anglers Rest for lunch and as we

came out Uncle Tom came staggering down the road waving his arms. His jacket was open and his shirt tail was flapping loose.

Auntie Mary stood watching him. "Look at the old fool. Just look at him. Well, I suppose we can't leave him in this state."

She held the car door open. "I hope you're ashamed of yourself. Drunk as a lord. And on a Sunday as well when you should be in Mass. Get in before I give you a kick."

He got in and said nothing. Clare giggled. I squeezed her arm and told her to be quiet. I thought there might be a big row ending with the *Gardai* dragging uncle off to the barracks if he was found to be drunk and driving.

Then Auntie Mary set off and after a few yards I began to think we would be better off with Uncle Tom at the wheel. I don't think Auntie knew anything about codes or road rules. In a buoyant mood now she began to denounce everyone else on the road as "fecking useless". 'Feck', as I quickly found out, was a popular word that had no relationship to the English word of almost the same spelling. And you didn't have to admit to using it when you went to confession.

Blarney, which we reached after repeating four decades of the rosary in honour of St. Christopher who, Clare and I hoped would keep Auntie Mary on the straight and narrow, was a very small village. There's a sort of square surrounded by little houses and just off the square, a castle. It was a grey, overcast day. It was a tall ruin of a castle and the idea of me going to the top made me feel grey and overcast too. I felt my mouth going dry.

Leaving the car and Auntie Mary at the gate, the three of us splashed up a muddy drive. There was a man there. He said we would have to pay him to show us around. And if we wanted to kiss the stone, it would be another shilling. We couldn't go in on our own as it was too dangerous.

Uncle Tom, a bit steadier now, pulled out a couple of coins and handed them over. There was a flight of stone steps up to the entrance. Puffing up them we went through the arch, to the right of which was a spiral staircase. We climbed four floors. All the steps were worn, covered in moss and slippy. At each floor was an arched doorway leading out of the tower and a little fence to stop you falling back down. The man told us there had once been wooden floors but the wood had rotted away.

The castle, he went on, was built by the King of Munster. Munster means the land at the bottom half of Ireland. This king had sent soldiers to help the Scottish people beat the English and to thank them they had given them a big stone which was called the Stone of Eloquence which, he told us, is a part of the rock which Moses had struck to get water for the Jews while they were in the desert.

When we reached the top, Uncle Tom was breathless with his face purple, and back drinking from a bottle he pulled out of his pocket. The guide told him he shouldn't be drinking as he could fall off. Uncle Tom told him if he didn't have a drink he would fall off. Then he sat down and lolled against the wall and shut his eyes.

"You lot get off. I'll wait here."

I looked at Clare who looked down at her father and shrugged. His face and his clothes were greasy with sweat. His chest was heaving. He looked for all the world as if he was on his way to the next one. I wondered idly how the undertakers would get his body down. Maybe they would just drop him over the edge?

The man, who said we had to call him Gerard, told Uncle Tom to stay still as he didn't want him to be killing himself. Catching mine and Clare's hand he took us over the lead on the roof to the battlements which were about about five feet high. He pointed to a big hole in the stone floor that went most of the way round and announced, that's the Blarney Stone. Well I couldn't see anything. Kneeling down he leaned across the hole, reached down and rubbed a rag around.

It was on the outside bit of wall and so low down you could hardly see it. It seemed sort of red and covered in snot or mould or something like that. I thought it was stupid and said someone could fall down the hole.

"Ah, no," Gerard said. "Because, you see, I'll be holding your legs."

Clare pushed past me. "Ladies first!"

"Good girl!"

Fishing in his pocket Gerard took out a belt and fastened it round the bottom of her skirt. "We don't want to be seeing your knickers, do we? You'll be nearly upside down."

She tossed her head. "They're clean and fit to be seen. Washed every Monday morning." That was the thing about Clare, she always had to be smart-arsed and have the last word. Sitting down she lay right back over the hole, wriggling lower and lower towards the stone. It was just as well Gerard, who was kneeling beside her, was holding her ankles firmly.

I felt my tummy squeezing up and holding on to him I leaned over to look. Past her head was a great drop down the castle wall and stinging nettles at the bottom but she didn't seem to mind.

"Give it a big kiss now," Gerard urged. "Pretend it's your boyfriend!"

Nuzzling the stone she gave it a big, sloppy one and her spit trickled over the stone until I could see it fall down until I couldn't see it any more. Pulling her back up Gerard undid the belt and smoothed her dress down.

"Now you'll have the gift of the gab ..."

"Oh, I've kissed it before!" Clare said, her eyes bright. "Can't you tell!"

"Well, wouldn't you know!" Gerard said laughing. "Now it's your turn, young man."

"Thank you but I don't think ..."

Clare looked at me scornfully. "It's no wonder you're running away from England. You've no guts. Spineless."

"I'm not. I'm not afraid. It's just I'm ..."

" ... a coward?"

Suddenly I felt really angry and the anger washed away my nervousness. Having done it herself she was all clever.

"Alright!" I snapped, lying down like she had done. Next thing I was over the edge and sliding towards the wet patch she had made. I gave the horrible stone a quick kiss, just like I used to give to Mum at bedtime. She used to call it a peck. Then Gerard, holding my ankle and shoulder brought me back up. I was a bit dizzy.

He waved a finger at me. "Now you've got the gift of the gab, young feller! You'll be able to talk your head off for the rest of your life. But if the gift ever starts to fade, we'll bring you back here and you can go over again!"

"That," I promised, "is never going to happen." My legs were trembling and I felt as if I'd rather walk twenty miles in bare feet over hot coals than do that again.

Chapter Four

After kissing the Blarney Stone I was a changed person. Whether it was from fear of being dragged back up that horrible tower if I didn't get over my shyness, or the magical power of the thing, I don't know but Uncle Tom seemed delighted with me. He became, as it was soon called, our agent, laying on bookings in a dozen or more pubs in and around Cork.

He made up an act for us. First I would be stood on the bar counter and I would read from the front page of the Cork Examiner. Nature had been kind to me and I was a brilliant reader and my performance was regarded as something like magic, or maybe it was the English accent and everyone thought it was great. Then Clare and I, standing on the bar, would sing a duet:

> "If I give you a golden ball that will hop from the kitchen down to the hall, will you marry, marry, marry, marry, will you marry me?"

Clare, who also had a good voice would respond scornfully,

> "If you give me a golden ball that will hop from the kitchen down to the hall, I won't marry

you, *etc.*"

The duet then went on through a series of things I would give including,

"If I give you a little black nigger, who will wash up the dishes and cook the dinner, will you ... "

Still she wouldn't marry me. Then came the last bit.

"If I give you the keys of my press, plenty of money at your behest, will you marry ... "

Then I would get a result,

"If you give me ... *etc.* I will marry you ... "

This, of course, got lots of cheers. But then I would counter with,

"Ha, ha, ha ain't you funny. You don't want me but you want my money. So I won't marry, marry, marry, marry, marry you, marry you ..."

Then there would be loud cheers and the money would clink into Uncle Tom's hat.

The act went on for some years and pieces I read out from the paper included news of the Sheffield Blitz in December 1940 which our 'agent', always quick with tears, exploited to the full. Then there was the fighting at Sidi Barrani, a name which sent everyone into gales of laughter even though I thought the British Army wouldn't have been amused. It went right through to December 1942 and the Iron Ring around Stalingrad which I also found puzzling as I couldn't imagine why anyone

60

would, or could put an iron ring round a city.

For a good while Clare and I thought it was great fun, particularly as we got a glass of ra-za for our performance. Then one day there was a big row. Clare wanted a new dress and her Dad refused to give her money to pay for it. She reckoned if he was making a steady income from the show and using it to support his drinking then she could have the occasional new dress. Auntie Mary was too nervous of her husband to join in.

I wasn't bothered at first but when he took my monthly half-crown postal order from Mum and exchanged it eventually for a sixpence, the worm turned.

Although an occasional plumber, Uncle Tom had been to technical college to learn his trade. That meant three years hard studying. And three years of books which were lined up proudly in a book case in his bedroom. Borrowing a wheelbarrow from the Shorts next door, I loaded it up with the books. I couldn't go down the Rock Steps so I took the long way round, along Blarney Street and over North Gate Bridge. The second-hand book shop was at the side of the Court House.

The shop owner looked curiously at my offerings. My uncle's died, I lied and my auntie has asked me to get rid of them. He opened a book and read the inscription on the flyleaf.

"Tom O'Reilly? And now he's gone. Poor Tom. God rest his soul!" Tapping his till he took a five pound note out of the drawer. "Your auntie will be pleased with this."

Well, auntie wasn't pleased because she knew nothing about it but Clare, who was in on it, certainly was. And Uncle Tom certainly wasn't. He didn't hit me though. When he was angry he used to sulk. Auntie Mary, of course, said nothing to breech the peace that she was committed to keeping in her house but in a few days a big basket of dried flowers filled the gap on the bedroom bookshelf. And that was that.

By now Clare, who was growing up, could wrap her father round her little finger. She had decided the pub act made us look like tinkers' children grubbing for money. So she was finishing. That was it. "Fed up of tramping round like a pair of eejits."

Uncle Tom didn't argue and didn't ask us any more and an air of gloom hung over the house. Short of the money necessary to feed the tills of John Rings he sat quietly by the fire lost in his own little world.

In the kitchen, Auntie Mary worked hard, assisted by Clare at her own money-making scheme. Ever since the government, which was short of grain, had introduced bran to the flour and turned it dirty dark brown, a lot of people had applied themselves to getting the bran out again.

In our house, a large cotton sieve had been made and for hour after hour the contents of the bags of bran flour, which were lying on the settle, were moved with the help of a large milk jug to the sieve where it was rubbed and scrubbed to separate the flour out. The bran was then bagged and sold to the leaseholder of the pigsties in our back yard. The new white flour packed in brown paper bags which Clare and I hawked from door to door in the wheelbarrow, made a nice little profit. Half of this Auntie Mary put into her husband's pocket. Keep the poor man cheerful, was her justification.

After a few weeks the storm clouds passed, Uncle Tom would come home singing his little ditties and Clare started disporting herself in her new dress bought with her share.

Most Sundays, when Uncle Tom wasn't too hungover, we would go for a walk. It wasn't so much for the exercise, or an excuse to miss Mass but to visit the tossing rings. The tossing ring was an institution where you could make a bit of money, or lose a lot. The rings were always held in the largest field you could find and had to be far away from walls and hedges which could hide approaching *Gardai*. The game was illegal and a watchman armed with a trumpet would be placed at any near crossroads to give warning of invaders.

Quite why the *Gardai* bothered with the tossing ring I couldn't understand but they did. Clare and I were not allowed to join in the activity so we would watch from a distance of about a hundred yards. I never found out how the game worked but it was to do with throwing money into a ring and shouting and cheering and sometimes fighting. But the real fun was when the *Gardai* broke through the security cordon and rushed like eejits across the field to arrest their prey.

The form then was for all the participants to race

off in different directions so that if there were fifty players and four *Gardai*, not much was going to happen. The *craic* was that the *Gardai* would be watching through binoculars until there was a lot of money in the ring and then treat this cash as pickings when its owners were away leaping over walls and stiles.

We thought it was a laugh anyway.

After the tossing ring we might stroll along the Cork road. About a mile out of town was a large white stone stuck at the side of the road. It was always covered in flowers or shamrocks and stuff. It was here that the Black and Tans had shot a young man who, so they said, had been trying to run from them. He was one of many who had been killed by these British soldiers who were called by that name because of their black trousers and khaki blouses. They had been active between 1916 and 1922 and the name was still used to describe evil and misery, just as the word *Gestapo* was beginning to catch on in the current war.

Dad told me that in 1920 when he was training as a doctor at the Mercy Hospital in Cork, he was arrested by them one night when he had broken the curfew by going out to attend a confinement. His claim he was a doctor was ignored and he was stood on the wall of Pope's Quay while the soldiers prepared their rifles. Just as they were about to fire, he said, a priest from the Cathedral saw what was happening and came and stood bravely in front of him. They daren't shoot a priest so after some shouting and threats they lowered their rifles.

Angry with frustration the sergeant had given Dad twenty-four hours to get out of the country and assured him next time there would be no priest to save him.

After a hurried visit home Dad said he carried his stuff down to the docks and boarded the Kenmare, a steam packet going to Liverpool. On arriving he caught a train to St. Helen's, where a friend of his worked and got appointed as a Houseman there, so he could complete his training.

The winters in Cork were mild. I only saw snow once in the four winters. As we came into Easter, preparations were made for the annual tattoo which was held at the Mardyke which was a large open field on the west side of the city by the river. After weeks of sawing and hammering, a massive structure resembling the General Post Office in Dublin was erected. It was in this place that the Irish rebellion, known as the Easter Rising, had started in 1916.

The Mardyke was lit up by searchlights when we arrived along with a lot of other people. There were stands round the field and they were full. The old Post Office looked great out there alone in the middle. After a bugle sounded, all the lights went out apart from one fixed on the entrance to the building.

Then there was a lot of shouting and a group of men, one of them waving an Irish flag, raced up to the door and battered it in with the butts of their rifles. Next the men appeared at the upstairs windows and started shooting into the darkness. Another searchlight went on and we could see soldiers on horses riding past. And then they were shot down and lay on the ground.

Then there was more shooting and soldiers running about. Some of them fell down. There was a lot of bangs and smoke. Then we saw big guns being wheeled into position. After that everything went mad. There was shooting and shouting and then more loud bangs and then part of the building fell away. Next it caught fire and the shooting got worse. Then it was night and all the firing stopped and the remains of the Post Office faded behind the thick smoke. As we got near the end there was complete silence as the voices of those left alive inside started to sing the new Irish National Anthem. I felt really sad then and I think a lot of other people did too as the song floated off into the night. A lot of people were crying.

At the very end, one light was left on and it focussed on the group of the IRA being led out to stand by a wall where they were shot and fell dead. Then I was ashamed of being English.

As we were walking home, a tall feller wearing a dirty fawn raincoat came over and joined us. Uncle Tom knew him by sight and called him Finnegan. Finnegan had a soft voice and it was difficult, in the talking of the crowd, to hear what he was saying. He was tall with long hair and a thin, hungry-looking face. He spoke quickly and looked round all the time as if checking if anyone was listening.

He seemed particularly interested in talking to me, commenting on me being English. I said my Dad was Irish so that made me Irish too. Overcome by the emotions generated by the tattoo I said I hated the English. Auntie Mary interrupted to voice the opinion that English Protestants were very kind people and it was the people in Whitehall who caused the trouble. Even though she was a quiet person, I knew she had strong feelings about The Troubles, as the fighting between the IRA and the English army was called.

Clare told me her Mammy once had a boyfriend who was shot by the Tans and if I looked inside her wardrobe door, which was something I wouldn't dare to do, I would see lots of little newspaper pictures of men who had been either shot or hanged by the English and that every Sunday night she would open the wardrobe door, light a little candle in front of them and say a rosary for the repose of their souls.

But now Auntie's anger was, I think, a thing of the past. It was as if the death of her little Brendan had sucked the life out of her and that she was only waiting for Clare to grow up and get off her hands before she joined the lad.

As we were walking along, Finnegan eventually caught me by the shoulder, bent down and whispered in my ear to come and see him. His house, he told me, was the little white one half-way down the Rock Steps and if I could come the next night at around eight that would be great. As I might be gone for some time I had to tell my aunt that I might be out all night. He wanted to know if I could do that. I said I could, as sometimes I went to stay with my sister who was living with Auntie Bridget at

Douglas and often stayed there.   Clare wanted to come with me on my outing the next day. She wanted to see Jean but I told her that as I was staying, she couldn't. She wasn't happy with that and spent the rest of the day pounding her piano until Uncle Tom, clearly the worse for wear from an afternoon at John Rings, threatened to slam the lid on her fingers if she played one more note. Then she went to her bedroom and slammed the door.

When I arrived at Finnegan's house there were no lights showing but as I hammered on the door a figure detached itself from a large shadow where the street light wasn't lit. Finnegan, still wearing his dirty raincoat put his hand on my shoulder.

"Can't be too careful, Niall." Unlocking the door he pushed me in. Sitting me down on the only chair in the room he closed the curtains and put a rather dim light on. "There's the barracks only fifty yards away. Bottom of the steps. You don't know who might be watching us!"

"Well I don't care." I was feeling brave.

"But you must, Niall. You must care if you're going to serve Ireland. You want to do that don't you?"

As serving Ireland was what soldiers did, I nodded vigorously.

"Good. Well you'll have a chance to do that now." Going to the window he inched the curtain back and peered out. "There's nobody there. The eejits will be playing cards and not taking any notice of anyone."

Going to a corner of the room he opened a large cupboard and took out a large school bag.

68

"You're going to school," he grinned, handing it over.

"At this time?"

"Well, coming home. You stayed behind because your teacher was tutoring you or you were in detention. That's your story. By the way, who is your teacher?"

"Brother Kenny."

"I know him," he nodded. "Ginger hair and a big spot on his face. Decent feller. He'll back up your story if asked."

"Why should they ask him?" I felt puzzled.

"Oh," he shrugged. "Just in case. Now, come on, no more questions. Pick up your bag and slip it over your shoulder." Going to the door he ushered me out. "And remember this is for Ireland. You're a brave man."

"Walk in front of me," he hissed. "Don't look back. I'll be right behind you. And if the *Gardai* stop you just tell them all about you're here because of the German *blitz* and the bombs. With an accent like yours they'll believe you. So just stay relaxed and friendly."

Completing our journey down the steps we passed the barracks and, as he said, you could see the *Gardai* smoking their heads off sitting round a big wooden table playing cards. There was a lot of talk and ashtrays and bottles of Guinness on the table.

Strolling over North Gate Bridge we went up North Main Street and then, on Finnegan's hissed instructions, turned right and went past the Court

House onto Western Road and up towards the university. As we got nearer the university I was hissed left and carried on until hissed to stop.

Finnegan then joined me in the dark and relieving me of my bag opened it up and did something inside. He closed it and handed it back. "Over there," he mumbled. "You'll see a war memorial thing to your right. Just put your bag by it."

Even though it was dark I could see its white shape, like a big tooth. I knew it anyway because it was only a few hundred yards behind the house on Magazine Road where another of Dad's sisters lived. That was Auntie Katie and she had four lovely daughters and I liked having tea with them.

"Just go and put your bag at the bottom of it," he urged. "I'm going now and as soon as you've done that little thing go off to Douglas. You'll be there soon. Remember what you have to say if anyone stops you. Go on now. And God bless!"

After a final pat on my shoulder he disappeared.

Going to the memorial I laid the satchel at the front of it. There wasn't another soul in sight. It was dark and I was cold. I couldn't read the lettering. It was something to do with the British Army but I couldn't remember what. But now I was feeling tired and Douglas seemed a very long way. I thought of sitting down for a bit but then started walking.

Ten minutes later, as I reached the Grand Parade an almighty bang ripped through the night and a flash lit the place up. It made me jump. I stopped and looked back but saw nothing. I thought it might be something to do with my bag but I wasn't sure.

Then I hoped it was.

As I was crossing the bridge to George's Quay a hand fell on my shoulder and made me jump again. "Where do you think you're going?" The voice was harsh and I could feel my throat tightening. It was a *Garda* with a big light stuck to his chest.

"To Douglas, Sir. I'm going to see my sister."

There was silence for a moment and then a sergeant came up. "What is it Dan?"

"This *gossoon*, Sergeant. Came down from the Western Road. I watched him crossing the Parade."

"What's your name?" The sergeant quizzed.

"Niall Murphy, Sir."

"Niall? Are you English, Niall?"

"I am, Sir. But my Dad's Irish."

"You're an evacuee?"

"From Sheffield, Sir."

He looked at me for a moment. "Tell me Niall, have you been setting bombs off?"

"Bombs, Sir?"

He shook his head. "No, I don't think so. Where are you going?"

"To see my sister. She lives with my Auntie Bridget in Douglas."

"At this time of night?"

"I was kept behind at school, Sir."

"And what school are you at?"

"Christians, Sir."

"On Wellington Hill? Bejasus Niall, it's a long way round you're going."

An idea flashed into my head. "It's her birthday, Sir. I was going to get a card."

71

"And where's your card?"

"The shops were shut by the time I got away from school, Sir. I thought there might be one open on Patrick's Street. A newspaper shop or something."

He stroked his chin. "Go on, Niall. Get off to Douglas. Your Auntie Bridget will be wondering where you've got to."

Giving me a pat on the back he turned away. "He's English," I heard him say as they strolled off. "He wouldn't have anything to do with it."

I arrived at Auntie Bridget's at about ten. I thought it was late but they didn't seem bothered. There was a salad and buns waiting for me on the kitchen table and a big glass of pop.

But I felt bothered. Not about being late but because of what had happened. If the *Gardai* knew it was me that had left that bomb I would be in real trouble. I suppose they could hang me. Or send me to prison. I thought of going down to the quay and getting on a boat to England. You could get on the boats any time as the crew were in the pub at night and often during the day as well.

But then I felt more cheerful after my supper and realized there was no chance of them finding me. After a little while I started to think that it didn't matter anyway and even if I was caught, Dad would take me away home. I lay on the bed in my own bedroom there and wasn't too worried.

Auntie Bridget was rich. Really rich. She had three shops on George's Quay and a cinema on Patrick's Street right in the city centre. The house was spectacular. It stood in very large grounds. It was called Ardmore. As you came in, the hall was marble and lined with white marble columns. There was a lot of gold stuff and a grand staircase. A long corridor off the hall went through the kitchen and had six staff bedrooms on either side. They didn't have any staff though. Auntie Bridget did the cooking and a woman came in to clean.

Uncle Mat was in one of the rooms off the hall. He was in bed because his legs didn't work. He had a tube coming out from the bed into a jerry pot and he used to wee into that. I thought it was a funny house with funny people in it. Mathew was the eldest son. He was going to be a doctor and had been at Cork University for a long time. He was always busy but I don't think he could have been very clever if he had to study so many years. Margaret who was his sister was a very nice and quiet person and so was Peter, the other son. Margaret would take me for walks.

Jean seemed to be happy there. I don't know why because I wasn't happy when I visited because I was like a stranger. I only did that because she wouldn't come to see me at Nicholas Well Lane as she looked down her nose at Uncle Tom and Auntie Mary because there were pigsties in the back yard. She really enjoyed her life at Ardmore.

The bomb had been on the news next morning and Uncle Mat was talking about it and asked me if it was me who had put it there. I felt funny but then realised he was joking, so I said yes. That made them all laugh.

After breakfast Peter took me upstairs. Auntie Bridget had bought him a projector and he had some films of Felix the Cat which we looked at. I had never seen a film before until we went to Auntie Bridget's cinema. She had told them to let Clare and me in free. So that was nice. But it wasn't as nice as having films in your own bedroom. I felt jealous of Jean because she could watch them every day. Then I went back home.

As I got in the door Clare came out of the sitting room, grabbed my arm and pushed me back through the door and down the garden. "That was you, you little fecker, wasn't it?"

My heart jumped into my mouth and I started trembling. "I've done nothing."

"Fecking little liar." I'd never seen her so angry. "You were with that Finnegan. You know he's IRA. Well, Bridie Ryan saw you on the Western Road with him last night. You had a big satchel on your back. And she saw you coming back down without it. Where is it now?"

I was dumbstruck. How could God be so unkind to me as to let Bridie Ryan be watching me at that time of night?

'Well?" Clare challenged. "Shall we go down to the barracks and tell them?"

"They'll send me to prison if you do that."

"Prison?" Her lips puckered into a sneer. "You're a real little fecker aren't you. Mammy looks after you and saves you from the Germans and the bombs and things. Well I think prison is appropriate."

With tears trickling down my cheeks I stood

quietly while she had her say. Then, to cap it all she gave me a belt on the ear that put me to the ground. "Now, let that be a lesson to you." She stood back and took a deep breath.

"Now I want you to help me get some dresses. I haven't got a thing to wear so you're going to help me. And if you don't, then we'll be going down to the barracks." With a final sniff she went back into the house.

I stared after her and then I turned and ran. I went down Nicholas Well Lane, up Blarney Street and across to Sunday's Well Road. I ran and I ran. Nobody was running behind me but I felt as if they were. Then I ran right through Sunday's Well until I passed the asylum and turning left ran down the fields to the River Lee. Then throwing myself onto the grass I burst out crying and pushed my face into the grass so nobody would hear me. At any rate nobody did because there was nobody around.

Suddenly I hated Ireland. And that came as a surprise. Of course, Michael had hated it from the day we arrived. He hated it because all the kids around called us Yankee Doodle Dandies. He had tried to tell them we were English but that did no good at all. All he got for his efforts was a punch on his nose which bled a lot. So after that he gave up and when he wasn't at school he just spent his time lying on our bed and reading or writing letters to Mum asking her to take him back home.

Up to now I couldn't understand why he was so bothered. But now I did. Ireland was a horrible place and they were horrible about the English and ... So sobbing to myself, I passed the afternoon away. In stories when children cry, someone comes along and talks to them but nobody came to talk to me and as I was getting cold I made my way back home.

Auntie Mary looked at me curiously when I got in. Uncle Tom was asleep and snoring and smelling of whisky in the sitting room and Clare was drawing some pictures of birds and ignored me. So I went up to our room, got in beside Michael and fell asleep.

The following day I felt a lot better. I had been dreading seeing the *Gardai* coming up the path but it didn't happen. I felt very cheerful after breakfast and decided to go and see Finnegan. But when I reached his little house I got no reply. Then a girl ran across from a neighbouring house and gave me a note. She said Finnegan had gone. He had gone up to Gurranabraher, to his cousins and if I wanted to see him here was his address. But, she added, I hadn't to go if I saw the *Gardai* following me.

Suddenly all my bad feelings were swept away as I went back up the Rock Steps and made for Gurranabraher. A picture filled my mind of Patrick Pearce and those others marching bravely out of the Post Office singing the National Anthem before they were shot. I could understand how they felt now. I thought I could hear a band playing in my head and bangs with smoke and I knew I had a job to do. That was to follow in their footsteps. To grow up and be a man.

Chapter Five

Gurranabraher was a council estate. It was really boring, as bad as the streets round my house in Sheffield. It was just there, long streets of it and being *Corpus Christi* it was a holiday and there were kids everywhere. The weather was as good as it ever is in Cork with the mists and fog that drift up from the harbour. The sun was making a good showing. Parents were sitting on kitchen chairs. Blankets were laid out on patches of grass passing for lawns. Older sisters were tanning themselves and showing a bit more of their parts than was decent.

There were the inevitable hurley matches with the puck whizzing round bouncing off walls, the green telephone box, the post box and when everything had been tried, off lads and the occasional lass who would announce their victimhood with screams and roars of protest.

There were prams with their innards removed being used as chariots, old bicycle wheels being belted up and down and babies all over the place whose Dads were snoring off their Guinness.

Finnegan's place looked quieter than the other houses. I knew someone was in though because as I went up the path a curtain twitched. Going round the back I knocked on the door. Finnegan's head popped out.

"Have you been followed?" he asked. He looked tired and his hand was shaking. Pulling me in he slammed the door shut. I was standing in a small kitchen. Through the open door was a sitting room. Everything was neat and tidy with flowers on a little table and a vacuum cleaner leaning against an armchair.

"Come in." He waved me through. Going to the front window he then peeped through the net curtains. Then he lifted a cushion off one of the chairs, pulled out a revolver and stuck it in the waist of his trousers.

"They'll hang me if they find me with this!" he said, patting the handle.

Before I could say anything he stood up again and squinted through the nets. "They can be crafty you know, Niall." Pulling a small bottle of whisky from his jacket pocket he took a swig.

"If I die, it will be for Ireland." His eyes were darting around and the way he was touching his gun made me feel nervous. "And what could be a better way to go. You saw those brave lads the other night. The lot of them were shot and ..."

He sat down, leaned over and tapped me on the chest. "It was Irishmen, Irish soldiers in the British Army that did it! Decent born and bred Irish lads shooting their brothers just because some English officer tells them to." He shook his head. "One day they'll all rot in Hell, I can tell you. All of them traitors."

"Now tell me. What did you say to the *Gardai*?"

"Well ... nothing."

He was sweating and his gun made me worried. Everyone knew that since the Civil War the government were brutal with people caught with guns. I had read The Riddle of the Sands and knew he had been put before a firing squad because of a revolver. Now I was with a feller who had one as well. I shifted uncomfortably and then stood up.

"Nothing at all," I said. "Now I've got to go."

"Sit down." There was another journey to the window. "I want you to do something for me. You were great the other night. And brave."

"I didn't know it was a bomb I was carrying."

He took another swig. "And what would you have done if you had known?"

"I'd have still done it," I gulped. "But you should have trusted me."

He leaned over and patted my shoulder. "But you were great. And you didn't say anything to the *Gardai* did you? I saw them talking to you on South Gate Bridge. I was following."

"I've already told you. Just a bit of chat about school, as you told me."

"And they sucked it up. God, you're a great lad!"

"So, what do you want me to do now?"

"Well," he shifted from his chair and scuttled to the window again, "are you mad at me or do you want some more work?" Coming back from the window he sat down again. "Do you want to make some money?"

I thought of Clare and her dresses. I had to keep

her sweet.

"Is it an IRA thing?"

His hand came down on my knee.

"What other reason could there be? You see, you having an English accent and you can get away with a lot. Like you did with the *Gardai* the other night. Now, what I need is for you to go down to the quay and talk to the sailors. I need information. Will you do that?"

"And where does the money come in?"

"Ah, yes." He took a swig and wiped his lips. "Half a crown a week. How does that sound?" Then another trip to the window. "It's for Ireland, of course."

"Go on then."

"You'll do it then?"

"What do I do?"

"Information, Niall," he said, animated now. "Names, cargoes, destinations. And when they're sailing. Secret stuff."

"Who's it for?"

He tapped his nose. "You wouldn't want to know."

"Shall I take it to your house?"

He shook his head. "I'm not there any more. Too near the barracks. Too many people who can't keep their mouths shut. They were there yesterday, you know. Came with rifles."

My heart leaped. "What for?"

"Me, of course. But I'm out in the country now. Past Dunmanway. I can't tell you where. But I'll be coming in to the city every day or so. I have my bike.

Then I'll see you."

Another trip to the window and a long look up and down. He handed me a little red notebook. "Write everything in there. You know the lady at the Rock Steps opposite me. Leave it with her. She has nothing to do with things but she's a good friend. She'll give you your money. And a new book when you leave one with her."

"What about the *Gardai*?"

"They'll soon get to know you, the English boy. You've already made your mark. The poor little evacuee. Just tell them you're a ship-spotter, like those eejits at the station writing down train names and numbers in their little books. You'll convince them because it's true, isn't it? The only thing they won't know is what you do with the information."

"What about ships with Gaelic names?"

"Don't worry. I'm not bothered with them. It's the others we want to know about."

Going to the back door he put the gun on the top of the dresser and held the door open. "Off you go now. I'll be in touch. God Bless! Saint Patrick will be looking after you."

His face looked like that of Jesus on the cross over the altar at St. Mary's. Sort of fanatical but sad and tired, only Finnegan didn't have a beard.

Clare was standing in the middle of the cattle market, hands on hips, as I strolled back down the hill.

"What have you been doing up in Gurranabraher? I've been looking for you. Mammy won't like you going up there. They're such a common lot."

"Walking."

"I don't believe you. Getting into more trouble, I suppose?"

I shook my head. "Just walking. Looking for conkers."

"Were you now? Show them to me then."

I don't know how it was but Clare never believed anything I ever said.

"Well, I've got a job for you now to walk to. They'll be paying you five shillings a week, when you're not at school. And that'll be my money, bomber man. Okay?"

I nodded.

"Over there." She pointed to the traditionally blood-coloured door of the local slaughter house. In fact, the whole house was painted red. In the old days the large square we were standing in was the cattle market. It had been moved taking its smells and gore with it to an out-of-town location and only Short's, the oldest slaughter house, remained.

Over the months since I had arrived I had seen cows and sheep being unloaded through its door and wondered what was happening inside. Now I was about to find out.

Clare pushed the wicket gate open. "Just ask for Stan."

Well, finding Stan wasn't hard because as I walked across the cobbled yard there was only one person there. A fresh-faced man with dark hair slicked across his forehead, he scanned me with raised eyebrows.

"I'm looking for Stan."

"Well, you've found him. Are you Niall?"

"I've come for a job."

"Clare O'Reilly was telling me about you. What school do you go to?"

"Christians."

"I've heard the brothers are terrible for the beating?"

"Only if you don't do what they tell you."

Stan's eyes twinkled. "So you get a lot of beatings?"

"No, Sir. I do as I'm told."

"There's no call to address me as Sir. I'm Stan. Right!"

"Am I to kill the sheep, Stan?"

He grinned. "Could you?"

"Maybe. If you teach me."

"Well, Niall, I'll not be doing that for the moment. You're job is more important."

He went off towards a large shed, beckoning me to follow. "I'm doing some killing now Niall. Just stand back and watch."

Picking up a sledge hammer from a rack he walked towards a door from which some mooings filtered out. Flexing his arms he called loudly, "now, Paddy."

As he did so a large brown and white cow ambled through the door. Punching a switch Stan turned a bright light on in the cow's face.

"See, Niall, I've blinded him. Now he can't see me."

Then he swung the hammer onto the beast's forehead. There was a cracking sound and the animal collapsed on the floor. In an instant Paddy and another man appeared and the cow was hoisted to the ceiling by its hind legs. In no more than thirty seconds its belly was sliced open and I gazed in wonder as guts and other things tumbled hot, wet and steaming onto the floor. The place filled with the smell of warm cowshit and stuff.

Within a few minutes it was all over. The meat parts had been put in a large cold room, the hide into the outside yard. The blood was hosed down the drains.

Stan rinsed his hands and dried them on his trousers. "What do you think of that, then?"

"That was quick," I said in awe. "You don't want me to help you doing that?"

He patted my head. "Not at all."

Going to a large bin he lifted out the cow's head.

"See here?" he pointed to the forehead. "There should be a bullet hole. It's the law. Poleaxing them like I did would get us fined if I was caught. So we have to make sure that doesn't happen. And that's where you come in."

He motioned me to follow him through the wicket gate and pointed down the lane. "That's the way the inspector comes. Nosey Bah, we call him. Looks like a bus driver. Blue uniform and peaked cap. He carries a case as well, a little case. If you see him with his case you come and tell me. Then I'll have time to shoot all the heads so he sees holes."

He explained there had been an ongoing battle

between the council and Short's slaughter house for years, with the council demanding humane execution. For Short's this was too expensive. Bullets and gun repairs ate into their profits, which from what I could understand, wasn't much. Lawful execution would put them out of business. But if I could warn them of Nosey Bah approaching they could hide most of the heads and shoot holes in a few for inspection.

"Can you do that?"

Clearly it was an important job and I felt myself growing taller. They would be depending on me and I wouldn't let them down.

"Next time we're caught we could lose our licence." he said, more serious now. "So it will be up to you. Next time we're killing, we need you on that corner keeping your eyes skinned. And there'll be five bob a week in it for you. Okay?"

It was an easy job. Old Ma Twomey's house opposite had a good doorstep and you could comfortably sit on it with a bit of sacking under your bum. Killing time was always between two and four o'clock. So it wasn't boring. And every Friday there was five shillings in my hand to keep Clare quiet.

It was after I had been in the job for about two months that things went suddenly badly wrong. I had been given homework about Brian Boru, a famous king who did a lot of wonderful things. There was a picture of him in my book dressed up in armour and waving his sword around. For longer than I should have been I was lost in the glory of his battle for Ireland against the Vikings. When I heard the screech of brakes and looked up, horror of horrors, it was Nosey Bah climbing out of the car with his little case.

I realised he would be in the slaughter house in moments. They had been killing sheep that afternoon, cutting their throats rather than bashing their heads in because they wanted the blood for *drisheen*, the sausage things made from boiling sheep's blood. There would be heads all over the floor, all waiting to be seen. Sheep, they should have shot also.

The car had thrown me. I'd not seen it before. Few people in Cork were driving cars because there was no petrol. It was gas bags that were all the rage and this inspector had one. They were about the size of a thick mattress and fixed on a roof-rack. You couldn't drive fast with them but they worked. Now Nosey was using gas to catch the Shorts out. He knew – they all knew at the town hall – what was going off at Short's but had never got near enough to catch them out.

Walking across the road as casually as I could I watched Nosey Bah open the boot and lift out a pair of Wellingtons. Sitting on the running board he took off his shoes and started putting the Wellies on. He was parked too near the gate for me to slip past and warn Stan and I was in a state. I would never be forgiven and Clare would get no more dress money.

Then a man walked past me smoking and quick as a flash, I asked if I could borrow a match. The moment the inspector was in the gate, I took out my penknife and jabbed at the gas bag. It was a sharp knife and straightaway I heard hissing. I scratched the match on the cobbles and lifted it into the stream of horrible-smelling gas.

The result caught me out. A bright yellow flame rushed at me, singeing my hair and scorching my cheek. I stood back in shock. A little jet at first, it began melting the rubber. Then it began humming, then roaring. Then it went boom. It made the dust on the road all round lift as if on a drum that had been hit and knocked me off my feet.

In no time at all there was a crowd and they were pointing to the back window Nosey Bah had left open. The car was filling with yellow smoky flame. I rushed to the slaughter house gate and barged through.

"Your car, Sir ..."

I put on a good show of panic because I was panicking. Stan looked at me dumbfounded. He was just getting over the shock of having the inspector on his premises without warning with some twenty sheep's heads on the floor around the corner, when I came in screaming with my head smoking like a fag end.

" ... your car is on fire!"

"Jesus Christ ..."

Pushing me out of the way, the inspector disappeared through the gate.

Racing into the shed Stan grabbed his gun and started shooting at sheep's heads as if there was a war on, while Paddy kicked others to the hole that went into the cellar. It took them only a couple of minutes to do what they had to but Nosey Bah was no longer interested. Stumbling back into the yard red-faced with fury, he shouted for a 'phone. Stan pointed him to the house.

"That'll be twopence, Sir."

"You little, fecker. I'm calling the *Gardai*," he snarled. He grabbed me but was stopped by Stan from banging me against the wall.

"It's not his fault, Sir. Leave him alone."

The worthy pointed at my head. Spittle dripped off his lips. "His hair is scorched, for Christ's sake."

"He was trying to put it out weren't you," Stan said, nodding furiously behind Nosey Bah's back, "trying to stop it, yes ..."

I started nodding as well.

"There you are, Sir. I think you should be paying him for what he has suffered."

Beside himself with rage now, the inspector forgot about the telephone call. Grabbing his little case he made for the wicket gate.

"You bloody Shorts, you've put him up to it. You've not heard the last of this. You mark my words."

Following him out into the cattle market we gazed at the remains of the Austin Seven, it's tyres burnt and smoking. Pushing through the gawkers Stan dragged the driver's door open, holding the handle with a hanky. A charred seat tumbled out raising a fountain of sparks which drifted up past the rooftops.

"My God, Niall," he breathed, "you don't do things by half, do you?" He pulled a pound note from his pocket and slipped it into my hand. "Go away from here. For God's sake don't come back again. You'll get me hanged."

Clare was waiting for me when I got back in. "Oh my God!" she shouted. "Just look at him!"

Auntie Mary came quickly downstairs, put her glasses on and examined my face. "You're burned, Niall. And just look at your hair. What in the name of God have you been doing?"

All the way home I had been fascinated by burnt hair falling down my face, making me sneeze. She fetched a brush.

"What if your Mammy was to see you now? What have you been up to?"

They sat down and listening with rapt attention, heard me out.

"And who did such a stupid thing as to set fire to the poor man's car," she queried, her eyes filling with tears. "They could have killed you. And what would your Mammy say to me then?" She was so distraught I felt quite guilty.

"Some eejit passing by smoking," I said finally. "He must have tossed a match towards the bag."

"Sure, God help us! What are we coming to at all. A lad like you nearly burned to death!"

"But I'm alright now, Auntie, so not to worry."

Clare, of course, knew I was lying and I hated her for it. She said nothing, however, until her mother had gone to find her rosary to offer up in thanksgiving for the miracle that saved me.

"Oonah and Noreen are in the attic," she

scowled, pointing to the stairs, "up you go."

These two girls were regular visitors to our house because they went to Clare's school, the Green. I liked it when they were around because, like Clare they were always kidding me on. Being two or three years older they were inclined to be bossy, though in a nice way. Like a lot of the Irish kids they were sorry for me being away from my Mum and Dad and I sometimes played on it because it made them behave nicely.

The attic had a pointy roof and was always hot. There was junk everywhere. Old books and things like golf clubs and tennis rackets. There was a pile of old cases in the middle the girls used as seats. In front of them was a collection of little glass bottles about three inches high. They were the sample bottles Uncle Tom used in his occasional jobs. After he had done a repair or fitted new pipes I would sometimes take a water sample down to the town hall where the Health Department would check the water was clean.

"So," Clare looked down imperiously from her suitcase, "sit there and tell us all about it."

She turned to her friends.

"This feller is the boldest boy you've ever seen. I can't tell you everything he's been up to. If I did and Mum found out he'd be on his way back to England as fast as the boat could carry him." She nodded her head vigorously. "It's the God honest truth. And now ... well, go on Niall, tell us what happened with the car!"

By now I was a bit overcome by the happenings

in the cattle market and was shaking a little.

"It was an accident."

Noreen snorted.

"You see," Clare waved her hand, "he's a liar too."

"I'm not ..." I started, " ... I just ..."

"Oh just shut up. The fact is you burnt the poor man's car. And what did you get for it?"

Fumbling in my pocket I pulled out Stan's pay-off.

"A pound. A measly pound. Is that all you got for saving his neck?"

I nodded.

"Well, we'll be seeing Mister Stan Short about that." She took the note out of my hand and stuffed it into her pinny.

"Now my little English cousin, I've got a job for you. Good money."

I stared at the bottles ranged on the floor. "Is it to do with these?"

Picking up one of the bottles Clare filled it from a jug at her side, put the cork in and held it up.

"Lourdes water. All the way from France."

"You're joking!"

"Maybe, a bit. But it is water. You can't deny that."

"How did it get here?"

"With the fishes, how else? You see, bright boy, tomorrow is the Feast of Our Lady of Lourdes. Lots of people will be going to the Cathedral for Mass. And you're going as well with our little bottles of water, shilling a bottle! We've got a little case for you as well. It holds sixty. That's three pounds! Then

91

we're going to Grant's. They've got a sale on. The three of us are treating ourselves."

"And will you be helping me?" I was a bit uncomfortable about it. "I can't do it on my own."

"No we won't and yes, you can. We can't go because everyone knows us. You're just a little English boy that nobody will ..."

Suddenly she stopped talking and putting her arms round her friends, started whispering. Then they started giggling.

"What is it?"

Oonah slid off her case, put a knee on the floor and stared into my eyes. "Have you just been looking up my dress?"

"No ..." I swallowed and started to go red.

"You're a little liar." She came closer until her nose was almost touching mine. "So what's that happening in your trousers then?"

As the girls were sitting in front of me talking I had peeked and seen their knickers. And I had felt that warm feeling spreading over my tummy. And I knew what was happening.

"You've got a stand on, you naughty boy!"

Shame and confusion swept over me. Their three grinning faces seemed to grow larger and larger, like balloons when they're blown up fit to burst, until I could see nothing but their grins. I got up and rushed for the door.

"And don't forget to confess it on Saturday!"

Howls of laughter followed me down the stairs to the landing. I slammed the door to my bedroom and lay face down on my bed. I knew now I really hated girls. Although after thinking about it for a while, I wasn't so sure.

A thin drizzle was coming in from the sea as I made my way to the Cathedral next morning. It was ten minutes to eight and people were pouring in for Mass. Lining my bottles on the wall beside the gate I stood back, took a deep breath and launched into the Lourdes Hymn.

"Immaculate Mary, our hearts are on fire ..."

The effect took me by surprise. I'd had many compliments about my singing in pubs and churches but on this cold, wet morning the reaction was great. The flow of Mass-goers slowed to a halt and so that they didn't block the pavement, they stood in a little circle around me. I was a great show-off and the attention spurred me on. One old lady, grey-haired and hiding under an umbrella was dabbing her eyes. Others just gawped. But at least I had their attention. When I had finished I held up one of the bottles.

"Just come in with the fish, all the way from Lourdes. Only one shilling."

What the fish had to do with it, I still had no idea but nobody queried it. A shilling was pressed into my hand, with a soft "God bless you!" And that was the start.

In no time at all I had got rid of the lot. At the back of the crowd I saw Clare cheering me on. Oonah was beside her with a couple of the North Mon lads. The North Monastery was the brother school to the Green and all the girls seemed to be very friendly with the lads there. I was a bit jealous but being a Christian's boy there wasn't much I could do.

Christian's boys were seen as soft and although the two schools were nearly a mile apart our lads seemed to have no problem getting into punching matches which the North Mon lads always seemed to win. I felt it was time I got going as well and picked up my school bag.

"Not so fast." A large hand clamped onto my shoulder. Clenching my fists I turned round to see a very large priest with a look on his face I didn't like.

"I'm off to school, Father. I'm late," I said breathlessly. But my wriggling was in vain.

"It's not 'Father', my son. It's 'Monsignor', Monsignor Burke. I'm in charge of the Cathedral. And now that I've introduced myself would you do me the honour of reciprocating?"

"Sir?"

"It means, telling me your name."

"Niall Murphy, Sir ... Monsignor."

"You're English. And what establishment in our city has the responsibility for your education, Niall?"

Opening my coat I exposed my blazer.

"So, it's Christians. And why aren't you at Christians now, Niall Murphy?"

"I've been ..."

"... getting money from people from selling Lourdes' water?"

"It's the feast day," I said lamely.

By this time, Clare and Oonah had scooted off with the North Mon lads in tow and I suddenly felt very lonely. Somehow I thought she would come forward and explain to the Monsignor but she didn't. It was her idea and now I was abandoned. I was right about girls.

Although there were hundreds of lads at Christians the building, once nine o'clock had passed, was silent as the grave. Led by my captor we went through the main hall, past the rows of silver cups to the headmaster's office. Here, to my horror, Monsignor opened the door and walked straight in without even a knock.

With his feet up on his large polished desk, a cigarette between his lips and reading the Cork Examiner, Brother Maher was also in shock at someone entering his Holy of Holies unannounced. And with a junior.

"Monsignor ... this is a surprise," he said, grinding out his cigarette.

"Is it now, Brother," Monsignor said, leaning on Brother Maher's desk. "And what about simony? Is that a surprise as well, simony?" He banged the polished desk to emphasize the word. "And outside my Cathedral!"

"Do sit down, Monsignor." Brother Maher pushed a chair forward, polishing it with the hem of his gown. "And you've got Niall Murphy with you?"

I was left standing.

"Indeed I have, fresh from selling bottles of Lourdes' water at the door of a church! If that isn't simony, I don't know what is. And from a Christian's boy, no less."

My brain was struggling. I hadn't heard the word

before. It seemed like sin but it couldn't have been because Monsignor enunciated it as though he was savouring it. It wasn't like 'murder'. Or 'sodomy', another word I didn't understand but which must have been really terrible as God destroyed two cities because of it.

"Selling not just Holy Water but Lourdes' water, Lourdes!" Monsignor Burke turned sharply to me. "If it is from Lourdes, rather than just courtesy of the Cork Water Board?"

He took out a large hanky and dabbed his face. I thought he might have been crying but he was just wiping beads of sweat off his forehead.

"May I have a look at this water?"

"Gone," Monsignor raised his empty hands as if searching for them in the sky. "He sold the lot. A pile of poor clowns handed over their money. Bought the lot, God help us!"

"And just how much money did you get from these 'clowns', Niall Murphy?"

I was surprised at how calm Brother Maher was with the intrusion. He could be a terrible man angry. I knew when he got angry he took his glasses off, for when he was caning, he could put so much into it they would fall off. I began putting handdfulls of coins on the desk, glad to be rid of them. They were becoming a burden in more ways than one.

"And this water, where did it come from?"

"Fishing, Clare said."

"And who is Clare?"

"My cousin at Auntie Mary's."

"Ah!" He gave a thin smile. "*Cherchez la femme?*"

"Pardon, Brother?"

"It means that women are behind all our troubles. And where did your cousin get the water from?"

"She said fishing. She poured it from a jug we keep in the bathroom."

"Fishing?" Monsignor was looking puzzled now.

"The fishing boats, it could be, come across from La Rochelle," Brother Maher began. "They buy and sell fish. The Germans don't mind that. And sometimes they bring other things. It could be supplies of Lourdes' water were brought in this way."

"You think it's genuine?"

Brother Maher shook his head. "How can we know, Monsignor? Perhaps it could do a miracle for us now, if only we had some ..."

"Well, I'll leave it with you Brother Maher." Monsignor stood up and tapped me on the shoulder. "And you bring your voice inside next time, to the cathedral choir. That's your penance. I'll be looking out for you. We could use a voice like yours."

There was an unnerving silence after the door closed until Brother Maher asked, "what do you know about simony, Neil?"

"Nothing, Brother," I stammered.

"It means selling holy things; blessings, penances for sins and all things spiritual. It's a bad sin." He fingered the pile of silver on his desk. "Nearly three pounds I would say. Will cousin Clare miss that?"

There was a trace of a smile on his lips.

"She was wanting the money for dresses."

"Well, I'm giving you the benefit of the doubt

and we are going to treat this as earnings from selling water come from Lourdes. We are also going to make a point to cousin Clare. So, pick up your earnings and come with me."

As I went down the main corridor after headmaster I couldn't be sure what he was up to. I had told the truth about the water coming from the jug and that the money was for Clare and felt in no position to contradict him. Reaching Form Three he tapped on the door and entered. The class froze.

"Brother Kenny, your pupil has been working hard this morning getting money for the Poor Box and it is I who have delayed him."

Brother Kenny nodded, his hands clasped behind his back.

Going over to the window Brother Maher lifted the small red box off the ledge and placed it on Brother Kenny's desk. He gestured me towards it and invited me to put my hand in my pocket again. This time, in the silence of the classroom I dropped coins into the box, one at a time.

"Now a big cheer for Niall!" the head ordered.

I was glad Clare couldn't see what was happening. She'd have killed me. But after the cheering I didn't really care what Clare said anyway.

Chapter Six

There were four English boys in our class. We had formed a gang in our first year because the Irish boys were jealous of us. They said Hitler would knock the shite out of Churchill and let the IRA take over England and this would be a laugh. They'd kick King George out and put Dev in Buckingham Palace and that it served us right after what we had done to Cork by burning it down.

Then we would start fighting and Brother Kenny would come in with a big, stupid smile and say in a soft voice, "now boys, remember Jesus loves us all. And England is the Dowry of Mary."

We none of us knew what this meant but as Brother Kenny thought it was a good thing, we thought it must be. He always had this silly smile on him and I thought he must be very holy because God had given him no other blessings.

But the fact that Mary thought we were so special that we were her Dowry, whatever it was, didn't impress the Irish lads. They would call us Yankee Doodle Dandies and sneer. And we would sneer back and call them stupid because Yankee Doodle Dandies came from America and that was in the other direction.

Sometimes we would fight in the yard when Brother Kenny wasn't around and one of them called Gus Flaherty, who seemed to be twice our size, would start punching us and they would laugh as the blood trickled from our noses. Then they would start singing "A Nation Once Again", which was a Fenian song. What a Fenian was I never found out but it seemed to be something to do with the IRA putting bombs into letter boxes in London before the war.

One day Gus's brother, Ben, who was in their gang, came in with a huge box of Turkish Delight. We all loved Turkish Delight. On the way home I sometimes stood outside Haji Bey's shop on McCurtain Street looking at it in the window. It was more tempting than the acid drops, bulls eyes and toffees Clare and I bought from the shop on Blarney Street with our Saturday pennies. In the Summer, when I got my birthday postal order from Mum, I went in to the shop and pointed to a little box. The man looked at my shiny florin and shook his head.

"You'll need a lot more than two shillings, boy. But," he picked up a little paper cup and dropped in two gooey pieces dusted with sugar, "you can have these." Leaning over the counter he relieved me of my florin and waved me to the door.

So how had Ben come by his big box? As we watched the Fenian lot gorging, Ben said "you see, we're not stupid. I won the money for being clever. Won it from Radio Éireann but I'm not telling you how. You wouldn't understand anyway."

He did tell us, of course. There was a programme

on Radio Éireann called Question Time. You sent in a question with the answer in a separate envelope. If the girl who opened the letter could answer your question you got nothing. If she had to open the other envelope for the answer, they sent you ten shillings.

"So what was your question?"

"You don't know what it was, then?"

"I wouldn't be asking, would I?"

"Well ..." Ben was really enjoying himself now, "I'll give you a clue. It's something you'll soon see a lot of in London."

"So?"

"It's a fylfot."

"A fylfot?" I wasn't bothered what it was or about his silly joke about London. What did bother me was that he had won ten shillings from Radio Éireann for sending his silly question in.

"So what's a fylfot anyway?"

Ben smirked. "A swastika."

"How did you ...?"

"You'd like to know, wouldn't you?"

"Someone told you!"

"No they didn't. I knew it."

Well I didn't believe him. Who in the name of God would know such a thing? It was all very puzzling. But it got him ten shillings and I was broke and Clare was waltzing around in different clothes and handbags bought with my earnings. I had tried to introduce the injustice to Auntie Mary, in a roundabout way.

"It's her Uncle Patrick," she said. "He has a big

farm at Farren. He's her godfather and sends her money for these things."

I gritted my teeth. Clare was a real liar but what could I do? Every time I came in she would have her hand out. "Cough up little bomber boy. How much tonight?" And I'd root in my pockets. Often she would feel me all over to check I wasn't hiding anything. I'd put a half-crown in my shoe once but it was no good. She only had to look at me to see right through me, like an X-ray machine. I'd given up the struggle. She'd won and that was that.

I dwelt on the ten-shilling problem for some time until I realised I had to do the same. The pay-out from Radio Éireann would buy all the Turkish Delight I needed. I would bring it to school and share it with the English gang. Then we could tell the Fenian lot to hop off.

There wasn't much to read in the house after the plumbing books had gone. I read a lot and got the books from the library; Biggles, Just William and all that stuff and there wasn't much in the way of difficult questions in those. And then, when I stopped thinking about it, the word came to me. The word I would send in was 'turd'. You heard it often in England but like bloody fylfot, it seemed to be unknown over here. A turd is a lump of shit. I looked it up in the dictionary and it was a proper word. It might not have been a nice one but it was there.

When you sent your question in nobody saw it until the envelope was opened on-air and this smarmy girl who thought herself so clever would read it out. Now, I thought, either she would know what the word meant but would be too shocked to say it on air. Or she would have to admit she didn't know it. If they got mad it would be too late because everyone would be listening.

I wrote my name and address and question on a bit of paper and put the answer in a separate envelope. I put a penny stamp on it the next day and counted the days to the following Wednesday. Auntie Mary was in the room when I switched the radio on. My heart was thumping. When Question Time started I said to Aunty, "I've sent them a question!"

She put her knitting down and came over to the set, as her hearing wasn't too good. My question was third. The first two were really simple and Miss Smarmy answered them straight away and sort of sneered as she did. Then it was my turn. I hugged myself gleefully as the envelope was slit open. There was a pause, then we were told that Niall Murphy from Cork City had sent in the next question.

"What," she read out, "is a turd?"

I was nearly wetting myself now.

"Well Niall, if you're listening. That's an easy one isn't it!" The sneering got sneerier. "A turd, of course, is more than a quarter and," she paused, "less than a half! You'll have to think of a harder question than that Niall, if you want to catch me out!"

Then came the punch on the jaw. "It could be something else, of course, but I think I have answered your question ..."

"Ah, yes!" Auntie Mary raised her glasses smiling.

"She definately got you there!"

The next day the classroom was in uproar over Question Time which they had somehow got to hear about. Words like Jackass and eejit and worse were bandied about by the Fenians. Even my English friends seemed embarrassed and didn't stick up for me. Fortunately I was saved by the bell.

Brother Kenny called for order. He walked casually over to me smiling, slapped me on the back and sent me to my seat. He then said he had an announcement to make and I held my breath. No, it was nothing to do with the radio programme. We were going to the pictures the next day, the whole lot of us. There was a good film on and Brother Maher thought we should all see it. It was at the Lee Cinema and we would be walking down over the bridge together as the weather would be fine.

We had been to films before. They were educational, like Dickens usually. Sometimes they were boring but it was great to be out of school during term.

"It's Gone with the Wind," Pascal whispered excitedly. "It was on the board outside!"

"Auntie Mary says it's not a nice film."

He threw his hands up with mock drama. "Oh, God ... so your Auntie Mary says we can't go ..."

"She didn't say that ..."

"Shut up, the pair of you at the back." A blackboard duster whizzed past my head. "Just shut up or my aim will be better next time."

The next day the older boys led the crocodile over the river to St. Patrick's Street. The Lee was on our left and coming towards the cinema from the other end of the street, on the other side, was a crocodile of girls. Our older boys began whooping and waving. The girls, from St. Angela's higher up the hill, pretended to ignore us but there were little waves from them.

Brother Kenny and two nuns positioned themselves at the entrance to the cinema. Girls were directed in left and boys right. The balcony was out of bounds. The older boys didn't like this separation and there was a bit of cheek and some manoeuvring, with a bit of encouragement from the girls.

Brother Kenny was doing his best. "Now boys ... can you hear me. Now ... boys, will you listen ..."

The nuns weren't having any of it from their charges, their grim faces and folded arms being all that was necessary to keep most of them in their places. After some of the wilder ones had been dragged out of the crush by their ears, the lads gave up.

They were a tough lot at St. Angela's and Jean, who had no choice in the matter of her schooling, told me that every morning after prayers they repeated the words "my crystal vase is unbroken, Mother Mary". This, I found rather puzzling. They had lots of vases at Ardmore because Auntie Bridget collected pottery and glass and stuff but I couldn't work out why people were so bothered about breaking them. And since there were about five hundred girls at St. Angela's I had a vision of houses full of broken glass. Jean, of course, said I was silly when I asked about it. It was a metaphor, she said.

Since I didn't know what one of those was either I left it at that.

Well, it wasn't Gone With the Wind. Moans and groans filled the auditorium as the film flickered onto the screen. A Christian Brother wearing a white habit and straw hat came out of a hut and was immediately surrounded by little black children grinning and waving at the camera. He introduced himself as Brother Patrick and said he was in the Congo. The camera showed jungle things like monkeys, screeching birds and long grass. He said the grass was full of snakes but we didn't see any. With a smile that reminded me of treacle he said he was going to bring all these children to Jesus Christ and his Mother Mary and we had the joy of being present at their baptism.

Then a big group of native women appeared, bare-foot and wearing only bras and long skirts and I wondered why all the bras were red tartan. Then another woman without a bra on walked in front of the camera. Brother Patrick waved her away and she went into one of the huts and all the boys cheered as her bits and pieces wobbled about.

There were hundreds of kids around Brother Patrick and he said to the camera we had to cheer each time water was poured over a child's head. They would then get a bag of sweets and their mother a bead bracelet. As the queue went back to the trees we reckoned we would be there all day.

After an hour of baptisms we were getting very bored. Some kids were jumping up and down and making rude noises. Lists of the old and new names of the black children we had been given as we came in to the cinema with the instruction we had to pray for them, had been turned into darts and winged around the auditorium. Brother Patrick carried on regardless.

Brother Kenny, however, got annoyed and finally came to the front waving his arms for the film to be stopped. This didn't happen and he had to shout how unhappy we were making Jesus who was otherwise enjoying the day. He didn't know that Tim in the projection room, one of my second cousins, had fallen asleep. He hadn't heard a thing, he told us later, until the *Gardai* burst in ...

Eventually Brother Kenny and the nuns lost control and in the semi-darkness almost the entire sixth form had shifted across to the girls' side. There were screams and giggling and tussles until finally one of the nuns ran out into St. Patrick's Street to find a *Garda*. As he blew his whistle at the front of the cinema, one of his colleagues turned the lights on and the entire gathering, with Brother Patrick still on his good work in the background, was ordered smartly into the street. It was here that Dominic, Gus Flaherty's elder brother and yet another of their gang, gave me a thump, stuffed a paper bag in my pocket and said quietly he would see me later for it and I had better not lose it.

By the time we had been separated and formed orderly lines along St. Patrick's Street it seemed half the *Gardai* in Cork had arrived. We were not popular. It didn't help that one of the girls who was almost hysterical, said one of the lads had threatened her with a knife if he couldn't have his way. The girls were sent off back up the hill with an escort, leaving us in neat rows with a crowd forming around us. One by one, *Gardai* searched our pockets while Brother Kenny, still red-faced with anger paced up and down, his hands behind his back.

It was inevitable I would cop it. I was hauled out of line, the *Garda* suspicious of the bulge in my blazer pocket. He pulled out the paper bag Dominic had put there and beckoned Brother Kenny over.

"What is this, Niall? What have you been up to?"

The *Garda* opened the bag fully. "Up to? More 'down to', Brother." Letting the paper bag fall to the road he slowly held up a pair of brown school knickers. There was a gasp from the crowd and I went bright red.

"And why is there a pair of these in your pocket?"

I stared, stupified. "They're not mine, Brother ..."

"Obviously," he remarked dryly.

The *Garda* gripped my arm firmly and said I had some explaining to do. I was to be cautioned and taken to the barracks.

"Not so fast, officer," my teacher said boldly. "I cannot believe this is young Niall's doing." He leaned closer to me. "So tell us, Niall, what are these doing in your pocket?"

I could see Dominic in the background, white-faced, his fist clenched and I began to stutter. I decided immediately I was more scared of him and his gang than I was of the *Garda* and had no option but to tough it out.

"I don't know. They must have got in my pocket

by accident ..."

"Accident?" the *Garda* said impatiently.

"There was pushing and shoving as we came out of the cinema. I don't know how the bag got there."

"Did you see who pushed you?"

"No, Brother. I don't know. It could have been anyone."

Fear was making me angry. And when I got angry I cried. Brother Kenny stood back, raised a placating hand and addressed the *Garda*.

"Alright. I believe what Niall is saying. I'm sure someone has just been making a fool of him."

The *Guarda* let go of my arm and Brother Kenny made sure I understood Brother Maher would be wanting to hear any new information on who might have placed the item in my pocket. I pulled out my hanky and blew furiously. Then I went home and told them it had been a grand day.

My brush with the *Gardai* frightened me. They weren't like Brother Kenny or my uncles or cousins. They could be really nasty if they were sure you'd done something wrong. I'd been lucky on the South Gate Bridge with a bomb in my satchel. I'd managed to kid them on after the explosion when I was the only person about. This couldn't carry on forever, as I was about to find out.

Uncle Tom, although never seeming to work, had a pile of plumbing stuff in the house. He kept it there because thieves often broke into his shop. Our front garden had became a store for his pipes, long, short, fat and thin. The sewer ones were the thickest, so thick they were too heavy to lift. The thin stuff was good for making tents and dens and Clare, if she was in a good mood, which wasn't very often, would help me. A few blankets or an old carpet slung over a pipe held between two trees made a shelter. And we would sit in it and giggle if anyone came looking for us.

At the end of the Autumn term, Clare went off on a class retreat. It was, she told me with that 'looking up to Heaven' look she'd seen in the film Song of Bernadette, to bring her nearer to God and I thought this was a good idea if it kept her further away from the money in my trouser pocket. But it left me bored with little to do, as I didn't really need to go down to the docks. So I decided I would do something useful at home.

The bottom of our garden was completely cut off from Nicholas Well Lane. To get into it you went through a door in the wall. The door let out a shriek when it was opened. One night it opened after everyone had gone to bed. Michael heard this hideous noise and woke me up. It was either a burglar or a ghost visiting us, he wasn't sure which but we pulled the blankets and pillows over our heads and lay terrified until Aunty Mary called us for school.

The brick part of the wall was four feet high. On top was a red painted fence that had quite a few holes in it. Dragging out Auntie Mary's step ladder I parked it in the garden near enough to the gate so I could rest the longest bit of pipe between the gate and the ladder. The plan was to join several lengths between the gate and our bedroom. If anyone came in again during the night we would be ready for them. We could pour water down the pipe, or perhaps ink so they would be marked.

It was a brilliant plan but I soon got bored again. The structure kept collapsing and I couldn't find bits to join the lengths. So I had a different idea. I moved two lengths I had joined so they ran from a hole in the fence to a tree in the garden and hid the step ladder behind the tree. Then I opened our gate and peeped down the lane to see if anyone was about.

I didn't have to wait long before a shambling old man appeared. Shutting the gate I rushed up the ladder and as soon as I saw movement through the fence holes on the corner I peed down the tube. There was a howl. My timing was perfect and as he was trying to work out what had happened I nearly fell off the ladder trying not to laugh. Then there was silence as he gave up and walked off.

This game went on for the afternoon and I thought it was hilarious, hiding behind the tree listening to the shouts and screams. Although it was winter, the branches were thick and even though one man peered through a hole in the fence he couldn't see me.

After a while, supplies ran out. Going into the house I got a big jug of water and drank so much my tummy swelled. I waited about half an hour and climbed the steps again ready to resume. It wasn't long before I detected another passer-by and my replenished bladder rose to the challenge. This time however, there was silence.

Hugging myself grinning, I waited for my victim to pass the holes further along the fence. Instead, I heard the shriek of the gate being inched open and held my breath. I dared not peek. I didn't need to. The *Garda* knew exactly where I was hiding. He was soaking, wee even dripping off his peaked cap. Without a word he pushed the ladder over and I went flying. He then dragged me up off the grass and gave me the biggest belt across the ear I've ever had. Then he left, all without uttering a word.

I didn't tell Auntie Mary what had happened and lay all night glowering instead. My ear ached and stopped me from sleeping. After chewing it over, I felt increasingly angry. Perhaps I shouldn't have been quite so keen with my prank but the *Garda* shouldn't have hit me either. He should have been keeping the law, not breaking it. I decided on revenge.

After breakfast I made my way over the river to Barrack Street to Auntie Katie's house. She was something to do with the council. She would surely help me settle the score. She was a nice, funny lady and when I showed her my bruise, very sympathetic. However, when I admitted to how it came about she became quite concerned.

"Let me see. Which ear did he hit?" She turned my head gently all the while making cooing sounds. "Was it this one?"

"Yes, Aunty." I touched it with my finger. Next thing a blow on my other ear sent me reeling across her kitchen.

"You pissed on a *Garda* ..." she said in disbelief, giving me another whack across my head, "... a

Garda! Your poor Aunt takes you in from the bombs. Looks after you and then ..."

She stopped suddenly and stood with her hands on her hips.

"Go back home. I've no time at all for you. You're an eejit. A complete eejit." She opened the door, held me by my collar and threw me into the street. "And don't let me see you again until you've got some sense between your ears."

Feeling really low now, I plodded down to George's Quay. Nobody in this horrible place liked me now. I sat down on the pavement and had a cry but as this produced not a bit of interest, I blew my nose, got up and headed off back home.

It was as I was coming up to the bridge I heard some shouting.

"Tomas Og has shot a *Garda!*" a man in the middle of the bridge shouted to a shawlie wheeling a barrow of coal on George's Quay.

"Tomas Og?"

The question floated back across the water.

"A *Garda*, I'm telling ye."

"Where, in God's name?"

"McCurtain Street."

"The right place for it then!"

"There's no good place for killing a man," the man retorted. "They'll hang him for sure!"

"They say he was a bit soft in the head."

"McCurtain Street is shut. *Gardai* with guns are searching for him now."

It hadn't taken me long to realise Cork City is really a large village. As Auntie Mary said, everyone knows everyone else's business. And so, I knew about Tomas Og. His real name was Tomas McCurtain. The Og stood for, sort of, junior. His Dad, also Tomas McCurtain was Lord Mayor of Cork during the Troubles. He'd been shot, assassinated by the Brits of course, or one of their gangs of hoodlums. They'd named a street after him. Now his son had shot a *Garda* on it! But what interested me more was McCurtain Street being closed. This meant there would be nobody on it, no one in the shops.

Racing through town I reached St. Patrick's Street and passed Father Mathew's statue to the bridge. It was true. On the far side was a *Garda* with a rifle. Jogging across the bridge I started up St. Patrick's Hill. The *Garda* shouted, waving me me back.

"I'm fetching the doctor," I yelled. "Mum's having a baby."

"Go round, by Leitram Street. You can't go this way."

Banking on the fact he couldn't follow because he was on guard duty, I ran. The man shouting on the bridge was right. McCurtain Street was deserted. Two other armed *Gardai* saw me and waved me away but I ducked into a garden until they were out of sight and carried on running up the road. I reached Hadji Beys and ran straight in. It was empty. They'd been cleared out because of the danger. Grabbing a big bag I shovelled Turkish Delight off the shelves and picked up half a dozen boxes as well. Then I was off. The *Gardai* spotted me again and started to chase but I was too fast for them. At any rate I think they had better things to do. I carried on at high speed up the hill then cut across to Leitrem Street and home. The bag went under my bed.

I was the hero at the end of term. Even the Flaherty's said so after receiving a big box of Turkish Delight. I gave one to Brother Kenny too. A Christmas present, I said. He seemed well pleased and I was king!

Clare on the other hand would get nothing from me for all the money she had extracted during the year. But when she got back from her retreat just before Christmas her X-ray eyes found the remains of my booty. I found her and her friends up in the attic making pigs of themselves.

Chapter Seven

Horgan's Quay was gloomy the following night. It was lifeless and it was cold. A line of silent ships were moored to the bollards by a cat's cradle of ropes which alternately sagged and tautened as tide and waves tried to drag them back to sea. Apart from the faint glow from their bridge houses, they were lifeless as well.

I was feeling very fed up. Clare had not stopped sneering about me being caught with a pair of St. Angela's knickers in my pocket and how shameful it was being associated with me. The cinema incident had gone all round Cork, it seemed. She hadn't heard the last of it at the Green and warned me I hadn't heard the last of it either.

She had also dismissed me as useless after I had come home with my pockets empty on the Lourdes Feast Day. And after all her hard work. As usual she was full of herself. Why had I handed over all the money? I could have moved it round my pockets as I was marched to school. I could have given half of it but no, and here she screwed her mouth up as if she was kissing a frog, I had to be the good boy and turf up the lot. The Poor Box! She was poor, she said. In desperate need of dresses.

To defuse her scorn I told her that money would be coming soon as I had found work at the docks ship-spotting. She was sceptical, doubtful that anything would come of it. She saw Finnegan as an old fool and me as a bigger one for letting him lead me along. But at the same time she felt I should give it a try.

"They'll shoot you if they catch you out," she observed airily. "Then at least there'll be no one left in the house to bother me."

So I got permission.

Standing like a fool at the docks soon got very boring and my enthusiasm drained away. I was shivering and Auntie Mary would be wondering where I was. I wanted to call it all off. I gave myself until seven and then, if nothing had happened, that would be it.

Stamping my feet I stared at the reflections of the street lights bobbing about in the whirlpools I made, like the swirling of the water as it hurried back to sea. After a while I felt quite drowsy. Then, just before my off time, I heard some shouting, then splashing. I strained my eyes and followed the river down. About two hundred yards away was a big rowing boat, a ship's lifeboat, coming up-river, its oars creating rings of dancing phosphor.

Its passengers were sailors. If they were coming up for an evening on the town the celebrating had already begun. One of them was playing a squeeze-box and a succession of songs drifted across the water with each verse followed by loud laughter. The boat bumped against the bottom of the jetty and as its crew came up the steps, I took a deep breath.

"What ship are you from?"

¿Qué has dicho? "What you want, little boy?" A burly man in a blue sweater responded, looking at my notebook.

"The name of your ship, Sir."

"Police, no!"

"I'm just collecting names." His friends staggering along the jetty called him. I persisted, "what name?"

"Oh, Alvarado, San Sebastian." He patted my shoulder. *¡Muy bien!* "Now I go for a Guinness!"

Well, I had made a start but reckoned at this rate I had a long way to go before I filled in my first page, not to mind the whole notebook.

"Now, why are you asking them questions?" A lady wearing a long, dark coat touched my shoulder. She had a nice Dublin accent, like Auntie Mary's. With all the noise and excitement I hadn't noticed her in the dark.

"Just collecting names," I answered, "like train-spotting. But I do ships. Er, it's more fun."

"What, you just stand here and ask for names?"

"And where they're going, if they'll tell me."

"Ah! A little spy!" Reaching out she took hold of my book and opened it. "You've not done much business."

I edged away. "What's it to you?"

"I'm Sister Ann. I'm a nun. I'm from the mission."

"You don't look like a nun to me. Nun's wear habits and have those things on their heads."

She smiled. "We're ... lay sisters. We don't wear all that stuff. What's your name?"

"Niall."

"Well, Niall, I want you to help me. Will you do that?"

I began coughing as a train came into the station on the next street, clanking, blowing steam, puffing a fog of turf smoke which drifted over the docks and made my eyes water.

"How?" I looked at her warily.

"We have a mission house just beyond the station. Sailors are lonely people and they often get into trouble when they're away from their homes. They're looking for friends."

"And how do you help them?"

We had moved down to where an illuminated sign offering sailings for thirty shillings to England lit up her face. She was good-looking and I could see she was made-up with lipstick and all that stuff.

"We offer friendship, food and drink. Relieve their loneliness. They feel they are with friends. Are you ever lonely?"

"A bit, at times. I'm from England and haven't got many friends here yet. And Michael's gone back home. He's my brother."

"And you miss your mammy?" She caught my hand.

"Not really." I pulled away. "They're all nice here."

"Who are you staying with?"

"My auntie and uncle. And Clare."

"Who's Clare?"

"My cousin."

She put her arm round my shoulder. "Let's go to the station. We can get a cup of tea and you can tell me about Clare and your auntie and uncle."

The buffet was only a couple of minutes walk. As we crossed the platform the Dublin train was still snorting clouds of steam and brown smoke and doing a lot of clanking. Nearly all the passengers had gone apart from a few waiting for the connection to Killarney. They were using the chairs strung higgledy-piggledy around the marble-topped tables piled high with cups, plates and dirty cutlery. Dragging two of the chairs over, Sister Ann placed them against a table, moved the pots onto the next one and went off. She returned with two cups of tea.

"Do you go to Mass?" She passed over the sugar.

"I go to Christians."

"So you've no choice. And all at home. They go?"

"Apart from Uncle Tom."

In the strong light I could see that although she wasn't young she was trying to stay looking that way. Her hair was dark and not tightened up like Auntie Mary's but tumbled down over her shoulders. Her face was quite round and she had a soft chin. But her skin seemed a bit stretched, like it was wallpaper.

"So how old do you think I am?" She gave me a grin. "I see you're trying to make me out."

"I don't know, Sister."

"Call me Ann. Sister puts people off." She caught my hand. "But you'll help me get sailors to the mission?"

"Why can't you do it."

She rolled her eyes. "Me, standing on the docks?

121

The *Gardai* wouldn't allow it. Too dangerous. But a *gossoon* like you would be safe. And we'll pay you."

"How much?"

"Half a crown for everyone you bring to the mission. And there'll be a drink in it for you. Tea or lemonade. And buns. Will you do it?"

There had been about twenty sailors in the boat earlier. If I had got half of them it would have been ... Oh my God! A fortune. Ten half-crowns. And there might be more than one boatload. Clare could have all the dresses she wanted!

"Come on, Niall. I'll show you where we are."

Leaving the station we crossed Glanmire Road and went down a narrow side street. "There." She pointed to a large, seedy-looking terraced house fronted with wrought iron railings. "Through this gate and we're there."

She rapped sharply on the front door. It was opened by a younger girl and showed a long, dimly-lit hall.

"This is Niall," Sister Ann said, leading me inside. "He collects ship's names. He's English, come away from the bombs. He's going to bring the poor sailors here for us."

The younger one looked me up and down. "God help us, Ann! He's just a *gossoon*."

"And this is Sister Angela." Ann spoke in a low voice. Kneeling on the carpeted floor she stared into my eyes. "I've got a brother your age. His name's Tim."

"Does he live here? I'd like a friend."

"Ah, God love us, Angela! Sure he's sweet, isn't

he? I could give him a cuddle."

She grabbed me before I could back off.

"So how about it then, Niall?"

They seemed to be really nice people. Very friendly. And the idea of the money was exciting. "I'm not down at the dock every night. I have homework to do. But I'll give it a try."

"Well that will be really great, won't it Angela?" She turned back to me. "Will you have a glass of lemonade?"

"No, thank you, I'm late. Auntie Mary will be worrying."

"Alright then and thank you for coming. We'll see you again soon?"

"Tomorrow?" I said.

"Ah, that's great. I'll be looking forward to it."

"I must be off too," Angela said. "Goodbye Neil."

She walked quickly down the hallway and as she opened the door at the far end, waves of conversation and tobacco smoke poured out and I could hear laughing. Then as it closed and all was silent again I felt the mission must be doing a good job making people so cheerful.

"They're full of the love of God, Niall. That's what makes them so happy. That's our job." Sister Ann put her arm around my shoulder again. "I'll see you off now. And remember, this is God's work. So it's like confession. We must keep secrets."

She opened the front door for me and gave me a little wave as I reached the street. "You come anytime now. God bless!"

123

It was really dark as I walked up Nicholas Well Lane. I felt really good because they were so friendly at the mission. Then I heard a hiss and Finnegan appeared from the shadows. Seizing my arm he pulled me into the scrapyard entrance.

"I've been waiting hours for ye," he said accusingly. "The *Gardai* aren't following you are they?"

"I've been making friends at the docks. They're really nice."

"Can't be too careful, Niall." His voice, low already, fell to a whisper. "Some of those people call themselves Irishmen but that's the last thing they are. They're just like the RIC feckers who worked with the Brits. Believe me," his grip tightened on my shoulder and I smelt his boozy breath, "they're all traitors. Every man jack of them."

"But I'm not."

"Ah, no. You're right." He eased his grip. "So what names have you got in the little book?"

I shrugged. "Just one, from San Sebastian. That's Spain isn't it?"

"But you've made a start. Did the *Gardai* bother you?"

"No, just a nun. From the mission."

"That's all right then." He looked around cautiously. "I'll shoot the bastards if they come near me."

"Have you got your gun?"

"Now don't you worry about that, Niall. Leave all that to me."

His eyes searched around. "I've something else I

want you to do. I'm going into the West on Sunday and there's a feller you need to meet. He's got a job for you. A very special one. I've told him all about you. Will you come?"

"Will I be paid?"

"Bags of money. Live like a lord if you do it." Pulling out his little bottle he took a swig. It's this coming Wednesday. It's a big job."

"I'll have to miss school. I could say I had to go to the dentists."

"I'll see you by Saint Augustine's. You know Saint Augustine's?"

"Next to where I sold Uncle Tom's books."

"Ah ... yes, of course. They buy school books don't they?"

"You see the kids queuing up outside."

"Yes. I know it. So I want you to go there. Go in and sit on the back pew. There shouldn't be anyone there. So then I'll come in. And I'll tell you what to do."

"Can you give me some money now?"

"What's the rush?"

"It's Clare. She's always on at me for some. If I can give her half a crown, or even a florin then she'll leave me alone for a while."

He gave a short laugh. "*Cherchez la femme.*"

It was the expression I'd heard before. "That's about women isn't it?"

Rooting in his pocket he pulled out a coin and handed it over. "Wednesday then. Three o'clock. Stay in your blazer. And bring your school bag. We're going shopping!"

A squeeze of my shoulder then he was gone.

I was back at Horgan's Quay the next evening, determined to make a go of it, not just for my little book to be filled but for Sister Ann's half-crowns. A few young sailors were kicking a ball around and without being asked, I joined them. As I played for Christian's reserves, I didn't make a fool of myself.

After a while we parked ourselves on some packing cases. There were a couple of English lads, four or five Irish and two Spanish who could speak good English. They were very bored, so when I offered them a free meal and a drink they were keen. Taking them along I rang the bell and when Sister Ann opened it I passed them over. I'll never forget the lovely smile she gave me. Two hours later I had another crowd and more entries for my book. I was making a fortune!

The next day when I took my 'tourists' to the door, I was invited in to join the others in the sort of sitting room that they had. It was lovely and warm after the bitter wind at the docks. There was soft music on the radio in the corner. Glasses of Guinness for the others and lemonade for me. Sister Angela brought out a guitar and soon we had some lovely singing.

As others of the sisters came in, one or other of my companions would get up and leave the room with them. Noticing my curious looks, Sister Ann explained they had a little chapel and the lads were taking turns at going for a few prayers. After an hour of chatting to the sailors and listening to their stories

I got up to go and at the door had a pound note stuffed in my pocket. Clare would be really pleased, even with half of that.

It became a routine. I would get a few lads from the docks and take them to the mission. We would have good fun, singing and drinking and then there would be a pound or ten shilling note in my pocket. The thing about it was that it was never the same lads. Ships came and left so quickly I had no trouble filling my book.

Then on the Friday it would be off to the Rock Steps to hand it in and get a fresh book in return. Not only was Clare doing well out of it but I had taken to putting some money in a little cocoa tin I hid under the pile of old things in the attic. I wanted a bike and didn't think Clare would agree with what she saw as a complete waste of good clothes' money, so I kept it a secret as she was always threatening to give me away to the *Gardai* about the bomb, if I didn't give her all my earnings.

Brother Kenny gave me permission to keep my pretend dental appointment on the Wednesday. I hadn't got a note from Auntie Mary. In its absence he looked me in the eyes and said he would trust me. After that I felt bad and made a firm decision never to lie to him again.

I had time to kill before my meeting with Finnegan so I strolled down to the docks in the hope I might pick up a bit of work. There was no luck there though. What with the cranes being busy, wanderers weren't welcome so I made for the station and munched gloomily on a bun.

There weren't many trains coming in. The Dublin ones always arrived after tea. But at the end of the first platform there was one train getting up steam. I watched idly large bins of turf being loaded into the tender. I felt weary. I think I was getting nervous about Finnegan's plans for me. The last one had nearly got me into big trouble. Would it happen again now?

I would have thrown it all in if it hadn't been for Clare. She was a bully. I knew she would snitch if I didn't do as I was told. And if she did I could be locked up. I'd heard about their reform schools.

Suddenly I was jerked out of my gloom. At the far end of the platform I saw Ann. And there was a soldier beside her. His green uniform made him stand out against the red carriages. I looked up at the board. If he was getting on the train he must be going to Galway.

Curious, I stood up and slipped behind a pillar outside the buffet entrance. If she saw me she might think I was spying on her so I squashed up against the wall. A guard came walking along with a green flag which he waved while blasting on his whistle. As the piercing shriek echoed round the station, Ann turned to the soldier, put her arm around him and give him a kiss.

At first I felt shocked. Nuns surely didn't kiss soldiers. But as he got into the carriage and slammed the door, Ann turned in my direction. I had been so interested in the performance I had emerged from my hidey-hole and been spotted. Coming quickly across she caught me by the arm and pulled me against the wall.

"What are you doing here?" Her voice was a bit sharp.

"They won't let me onto the quay because of the cranes working so I came here."

"That's alright then." She gave me a funny sort of smile. "I was just seeing my brother off. He's in the army. Going up into Galway." She paused. "Would you like to be a soldier, Niall?"

I shook my head. "My Dad says I'm going to be a doctor."

"Well, that would be grand wouldn't it?" She kept looking around, sort of jerking her head. Then suddenly she bent over and kissed my forehead. "Now that's two men I've kissed today. Aren't I a wanton?"

Before I could answer, she was off. "Will we be seeing you tonight?" she called over her shoulder.

My reply was drowned by the whistle of the departing train.

I reached St. Augustine's on the dot. I'd not been in the place before but I thought it was lovely. Instead of the usual gloominess of Irish churches it was big and bright and the floors and pews highly-polished and the light from large windows filled it with a cheerful glow. As it was empty I yielded to temptation and racing down the aisle, skidded the last twenty yards and banged into the altar rails. As a penance I lit a candle under the statue of St. Augustine who was looking disapprovingly from his niche.

Then I sat down at the back and waited.

"Niall!" a whisper pulled me out of my reverie. Standing at the end of the pew a tall priest with a black, broad-brimmed hat was beckoning me.

"Father?"

"It's me you silly arse!" Taking off his hat, Finnegan gave a mocking bow. Where he had got the cassock from, I don't know but it quite suited him. "Quick. Into the confessional. As if you want to tell me your sins!"

Striding off down the aisle he turned into the confession box, opened the door of the priest's side and stepped in. Since the church was empty I wasn't shy either. I opened my door and knelt down automatically. As I did, the little light came on and the screen slid back.

"You've made it then. Good man. Now, we must hurry. Are there any books in your satchel?"

Unstrapping it I showed him it was empty apart from a bit of newspaper my dinner had been wrapped in. He pulled a brown paper bag from under his cassock and took out a pair of pliers and a little brown thing like a dead mouse without a head. Opening the pliers he placed the jaws over the sausage thing and squeezed. I heard a distinct crack like glass breaking. Reaching through the hatch he dropped the thing into my satchel. He did the same thing three more times and soon my satchel was half full.

"Okay?" He looked at me. "Now fasten your bag up. Don't tip it and go outside and wait for me."

"What are they?"

He wagged a finger. "Ask no questions, Niall. Just do it." Crumpling the paper bag up he stuffed it under his cassock again, pulled out his little bottle and took a swig.

A woman was waiting as I left the box. "Is Father still in?"

She brushed past me, went in and shut the door. As she did, Finnegan clicked his light off and came out. The penitent's door reopened.

"Father ... ?"

"I'm sorry, Missus. I have to see the Bishop." Ignoring her imploring gaze he swept down the aisle and went outside.

When I joined him he was still grinning. "If it had been a sweet young *colleen* I might have listened to her sins and given her, well, God knows what penance! But she was too old." He put his arm around my shoulder. "Now, we're going to the Grand Parade. Paying a visit to Grant's. Time for them to do a bit of penance."

As you enter the Parade, Grant's is straight ahead. Four stories high and the length of four ordinary shops it dominates the others. Uncle Tom said there was something funny about Grant's because when the Black and Tans had burned the city centre they had by-passed a juicy target. What he meant by 'funny' he never explained but I felt it was ominous in some way.

As we went through the door a man in a uniform saluted. "Can I help you Father?"

"God bless you, my Son. It's uniforms, for my nephew, I'm after. A Christian Brothers College uniform for him. And I'm looking for furniture. They're moving me out west shortly and I have a parish house to furnish."

While the commissionaire gave instructions to where 'Father' Finnegan could find what he wanted, I drifted off. The place was full of ladies, many towing pretty-looking daughters. For a laugh I went and stared at them. They were looking at knickers and stuff and I was glowered at.

Finnegan soon put a stop to that. Coming up behind he grabbed my arm and dragged me away.

"Now look," he whispered, "we'll be in here a while and I don't want you attracting unnecessary attention. Just follow me round and do what I say. Leave the pretty girls for another time."

The next hour or so was really boring. Finnegan talked to everyone, putting on a great show. Bedroom furniture, curtains, armchairs, clothes, on and on he went. Every time they called him 'Father' I wanted to laugh. But he knew how to carry it off.

Going down to the ground floor pretending to be looking for, God only knows what, he nudged me towards a pile of boxes and stuff behind a staircase and whispered I was to stand still and not look round. I did what he said and felt him undoing my satchel and messing around. Nobody took any notice of him at all. They must have been getting fed up with his endless questions. This business of 'stand still and don't look round' happened several more times until a lady in a black overall came over to us.

"It's closing time, Father."

"Oh my God!" Finnegan sounded surprised, then he took a deep breath. "Well, I haven't finished yet. But I can come back tomorrow afternoon."

The assistant shook her head. "We'll be closed, Father. It's Thursday. Come on Friday. And we'll be happy to help you."

"Closed? Well, Friday it will have to be. Come along, Niall." He steered me towards the door and muttered, "but I don't think we'll be coming back ..."

"Why won't we be back, what were those things?"

"You know what stink bombs are!" he said grinning. "They give off a horrible smell. It'll drive their customers away. Smell all their merchandise. It'll be a laugh won't it?"

"But why have we been doing it?"

We turned down past the Court House and the noise of traffic of people going home faded.

"They wouldn't pay up. All that money they have and they can't spare a bit for us. So it's been decided they learn a lesson ..."

We stopped outside a toilet. He patted my back looking really pleased with himself. "Go off home now. You've done a great job. Pearce would be proud of you. And whatever happens, not a word. Not a single word ... And we'll still be looking for your reports on the ships. That's where your money will come from. You're going to make Clare very happy soon. Very happy indeed!"

I turned at the end of the street and saw him come out of the toilet without his priest's clothes. Then he was gone.

When I got in from school the next day Auntie Mary was waiting. "Clare's at her piano lesson. It's getting a bit dark now Niall. Could you go down there and walk home with her?' She handed me two pennies. "There now, there's one for the both of you. You can buy some sweets on the way back."

With all the money I had secreted away one penny counted for little. But if I'd ever loved anyone, apart from myself maybe, it was Auntie Mary. So I didn't laugh. I hated it if I upset her. Taking the money I set off down the lane.

Clare's piano teacher lived at the top of the Rock Steps. I was there in a few minutes and slipping in, I sat on the couch watching Clare struggling. She wasn't a good player but she fancied herself and of course, piano teachers have good reasons for not bringing this to the attention of their pupils. I had tried to enlighten her but got little for my efforts apart from a promise of a belt on the ear if I didn't keep my opinions to myself.

The teacher's house fronted the little road and suddenly there were yells and running of lots of feet. Then a voice shouted "my God, there's a fire!"

That ended the piano lesson. Clare and her teacher jumped up and rushed by me to the door. For some reason that I can't put a finger on, or more likely didn't want to, I didn't have the same sense of urgency. It was like in the films where the background music slips into creepy before the ghost appears. It took a few more 'oh, my Gods!' to get me to my feet.

The teacher's house was the end one of a row of

six. Then there was a drop of about two hundred feet to the quay. The pavement was edged with iron railings and it made a great viewing stand, like a high pulpit. I stood with what seemed to be the whole of Blarney Street yelling and oo-ing and ah-ing at Cork city below us. The sun had gone and a soft blue mist was rising from the quays and rivers.

There was no missing the area of interest in the middle of the city. It was too dark to tell precisely where the fire was but a long yellow flame like a candle's was snaking and curling, trying to reach the clouds that were so low they showed its reflection. I went numb. The flames were like a Cobra moving from side to side mesmerised by the sound of a scruffy-looking man with a turban playing a flute.

"It's Grant's!"

The shout echoed up the steps. Two lads, their faces shining with excitement came rushing up two at a time as I lost control of my bladder. The trickling noise reached Clare beside me. She looked down, screamed and stepped away.

"Jesus Christ, Niall, you're pissing yourself ..."

She looked at me for a few moments and when the stream ceased, came back glaring. "It's you, you little fecker," she said in an angry whisper, gesturing across the city. "It's you that's done this!"

Tears rolled down my cheeks. Everyone else was too busy enjoying the disaster to take any notice but grabbing my arm she pulled me away from the gathering and up Blarney Street which was quite empty.

"You were in Grant's yesterday. I heard you telling

Mammy. Was that eejit with you?"

I nodded and wiped away my tears with my sleeve. "He said it was just stink bombs to teach them a lesson."

She stared at me again her eyes flashing. "Right," she spoke very decisively. "I'm going to tell Mammy. And she'll tell the *Gardai* and you will go to prison."

Catching hold of her cardigan I pulled her back. "I'll pay," I said in desperation.

"Pay?" she snorted. "Not for all the money in the world."

"I've got five pounds."

"Five pounds?" She lowered her music case onto the pavement and folded her arms. "And where in God's name did you get that sum of money? Five pounds. I don't believe it."

"It's in the attic. I've hidden it."

"I thought I had all the money you got from your ship-watching?"

"You have," I spoke earnestly. "But the Sisters have been giving me money too."

Her voice lowered conspiratorially. "What Sisters, Niall?"

"I don't know. They run a mission for seamen and for every sailor I bring them they give me half a crown."

"And you never told me?"

"I ... wanted a bike."

"So you were cheating me. And lying?"

"I suppose so."

"Suppose? You suppose so? Well let me tell you," her eyes flashed as she stabbed her finger at me, "there's no 'suppose' about you being a liar. That money's mine. It's for keeping my mouth shut about the bomb."

"If the *Gardai* take me away there'll be no money at all. And the five pounds will stay hidden. You'll never find it." I was thinking on my feet.

She ran her fingers through her hair for a moment. "Alright then, alright Niall Murphy. So, we'll have to make sure they don't take you away."

"You'll do that?" Relief surged over me.

Clare ran her finger down her left breast and then across. "Cross my heart. Even though you are a liar, I'll not tell. But don't you forget you owe me now for the bomb and the fire. When can I have my money?"

"When we get home."

"Okay. And now," she pulled out a florin from her pocket and waved it gleefully, "I didn't have my full lesson due to her rushing off. So, we'll buy some chips!"

The following morning I felt great. Quite proud of what I, what we had done. I felt that Patrick Pearce would pat me on the shoulder and give me a nod of approval. I was a hero. You couldn't tell people that though. They'd even sneered at Pearce and the others as they came out of the Post Office.

I remember Uncle Tom telling us that as they had been led away by the Brits, one old woman had lashed out and shouted "they ought to execute you all and then give you a kick up the arse!" He had nearly fallen over laughing at this. But Pearce and the other lads were shown to be right in the end.

I took the long way to school, up North Main Street and along Patrick Street. There were a large number of onlookers in the Grand Parade. From a distance it looked as if the front wall was about to collapse and the firemen had put a rope barrier up to warn the gawkers off.

'If only they knew it was me' I thought, feeling really smug. But no, I'd have to hide my glory. Five pounds was a lot to pay for Clare's silence. But without it I'd be ... well, I didn't want to think about that.

A hundred yards or so down Patrick Street I turned into a little alley. At the end was the staff entrance to Grant's, a small door in the wall. I used to wait there when meeting my cousin Margaret who worked in the store. She would take me home to tea in Douglas and then we'd go to the Lee Cinema which, because, it was owned by Auntie Bridget, we were allowed in for free.

Now the door to the staff entrance was gone. Sidling up to it I looked in. God, it was a mess. The roof had fallen in all the way to the cellar. Above, only a few slates and charred beams remained. There were piles of ash and a horrible smell.

"Go away sonny." A fireman waved me off. "It's dangerous here."

At that moment a *Garda* came down the alley towards me. My heart jumped for a moment but I don't think he even saw me. He had some stuff on his shoulder and I think he was a Superintendant or whatever they call them.

"Anything, Paddy?"

The fireman touched his helmet and shook his head. "Nothing at all. All we know is it started on the ground floor. But everything's gone now. Not a chance of any clues."

"So ... ?"

"Well," the fireman shrugged, "could be electric. It could have been a smouldering cigarette end. We'll never know."

I felt like laughing. I could imagine going up to the two of them and saying, "well, I know" and I thought of how they would look at me. But I knew Clare would be mad if I did that. So I just turned away and went off to school.

Chapter Eight

There were sparks bursting like fireworks and flames and walls crashing down on me; and water from the hoses cutting arcs through the sky and looking very pretty, glittering like diamonds; the noise of the engines sucking water out of the river and pushing it up Grand Parade through squiggling pipes was overwhelming; crowds gaped at me. And what if there had been people in the store ...?

Night after night these dreams wouldn't go away. Some nights I don't think I slept at all and after a few spoonfuls of cornflakes I would rush off with Auntie asking if I was alright. Somehow, things got better when I walked, so I walked a lot. One night after tea I walked all the way to Douglas to see Jean but on arriving at Ardmore I turned and walked back. She would have known something was up. I was now paying the price for what I had done.

One afternoon I was lying on the floor doing some drawing and wasn't feeling very good. Clare was practising on the piano and I thought I would have a laugh. Creeping slowly across the floor behind her I reached under the piano stool and was about to press the soft pedal when she screamed.

She also jumped up so fast she knocked the piano stool over. I was immediately accused of getting under the stool so I could look up her dress. It wasn't true but as Auntie Mary came rushing down the stairs I knew I was in trouble. She glanced at her sobbing daughter, came straight up to me and for the first and only time, gave me a belt.

About a fortnight after the fire I was feeling really awful. Lying in bed I wriggled and turned. I thought maybe if I went down to the quay and got on a boat going to England, things would get better. But there were lots of stowaways trying that. It wasn't escape they wanted but a job. Everyone talked of the money to be earned in the factories around Birmingham and when they got there it was true, six pounds a week, for God's sake!

There were Germans trying to get to England as well. Submarines or fishing boats would bring them into Cobh. Then, with dynamite in their suitcases, they would make for the English boat and hope to cause big trouble once they arrived and got into a factory.

Dev wasn't having any of it. Every time a boat was loading now, *Gardai* would stand on the gangways and question the passengers and search their bags. So what chance would I have? At times my head felt as if it was bursting. I would cry softly to myself. I could have gone down to Pope's Quay and jumped into the River Lee but that would be suicide, a mortal sin. I would burn in hell. Besides, the water was cold.

On the Sunday morning I woke up trying to

scream. I couldn't breath. It was as if a belt was tied round my chest. My throat felt roaring hot. And as it got worse I couldn't make any sounds at all. I just lay there gurgling. Then I think I fainted because the next thing I heard was Auntie Mary shouting for Billy in the end bedroom to go next door to Short's and get on the 'phone for an ambulance. I heard Billy jump up and the clatter of his feet down the stairs.

After that, things began to fade. I still had the pain around my chest and the burning sensation. I remember being carried down the path. Although it was early in the morning there were people round the ambulance saying things like "Sweet Jesus!", "have mercy on him!" and "Mother Mary, protect your child!", and so on. Then off we went.

Next I was in a ward. There were nurses standing around my bed and a couple of doctors in white coats. They were looking at me, talking. Auntie Mary was sitting across the corridor by the door. I think they had told her she couldn't come in. Then I had a mask pushed onto my face. I hated that and started struggling but then I heard gas hissing and felt a bit better.

Later on – I really had no idea of time – a priest came in and put a little candle on the locker beside my bed. After lighting it he put a thing round his neck, a long sash which he kissed. Then he opened a little bottle and poured something onto a wad of cotton wool and rubbed it onto my forehead, my chest and my feet. While he was doing that he talked in Latin and then he opened a little gold box, took out a communion wafer and was about to put it into my mouth when a doctor came and told him not to as it might choke me.

He turned to the Doctor, eyebrows raised. "The body of Christ?" Then he broke the host in half and half again and more until he had a piece the size of a grape pip on his finger end. He leaned forward.

"*Corpus domini nostril ...*" and placed it on my tongue.

Then Auntie Mary came over and talked to the doctor. I heard her say my mother was in hospital and very ill and the English police had told my father he couldn't travel to Ireland as they were expecting an air raid in Sheffield and he would be needed in the hospital.

That didn't bother me. I didn't want to see them anyway as they had been so horrible to me. I thought they would be sad when I was dead and would realize how awful they had been.

I had this picture of them standing round my bed, which would be covered in flowers, just like little Theresa's had been. She was a girl I played picky with on the lane a year before. It was a kind of hopscotch where you had to hop over chalked squares knocking an empty Vaseline jar which was filled with sand.

Well, it seems that Theresa had hopped too much because as she had landed with a bump, her lungs burst and blood had come out of her mouth. They said it was consumption and Auntie Mary had taken me to the wake. And someone had read a poem like "consumption has no pity for blue eyes and golden hair."

Everyone was crying as they looked at Theresa lying there on her bed. There were candles everywhere and flowers. And everyone was saying the rosary for her soul. I thought that was silly because I knew Mother Mary would be sad that she had died and right now would be holding her in her arms, so saying a rosary was a waste of time.

Then I had gone downstairs. They had a lot of sandwiches and buns on the table and I had sat eating them until Auntie came down and told me for some reason to go back home and that I was a disgrace.

But, even though I had the gas there in the hospital I didn't feel that much better. It was still hard to breath and I was sore around my waist. And every time I sucked in, the sore became a pain. It was so bad I didn't want to bother breathing any more and just gave little gasps. Lots of black spots floated in front of my eyes and when I told the nurse she just said "don't worry" and went off for the doctor. When he came in, Auntie Mary was still there beside me and I could hear them whispering but it was very clear. I had something called *status asthmaticus* and it was a problem but they were working out what they could do.

Shortly after that the ward door opened and two men came in wheeling a trolley. On the trolley was a coffin. When I saw that I caught Auntie's hand and started crying. She said I wasn't to be afraid. She laughed when I called it a coffin but I think she was just putting it on.

They put the coffin on the bed next to me and pulled out some wires which they put into a plug. Sitting down on the other side of my bed the doctor told me that what I thought was a coffin was an iron lung. They called them that because the first ones, which were made in America, were iron. But this one was made of wood and it was just as good. He said they were using it because my muscles were getting tired of trying to get me to breath and when I lay down inside it, a pump would do all the hard work and give the muscles in my chest a rest so they could become strong again.

Pulling back the blankets two nurses lifted me across and placed me inside the thing. There was rubber on the bottom so it was quite comfortable. Then they put the lid down leaving me with my head stuck out just like I saw in a circus when they put this girl in a box and sawed her in two. They wrapped a sort of scarf round my neck and switched the thing on.

At first it was really frightening as my body started to swell. My chest muscles were pulled up and that was really uncomfortable. But, as Auntie Mary held my hand, I felt myself starting to breath really deeply. My head stopped being fuzzy and the black spots went away.

"There now, Niall. You're on the mend."

"Will I have to stay in this thing all the time?"

"You're only in there because the tubes to your lungs have squeezed shut and air can't get in. The next thing they're going to do is get those tubes to open up again. Then you can come out."

"What about having a wee?"

"Oh," Auntie laughed, "the nurses can help you there. Don't worry. It's their job!"

Well, I soon wanted a wee and when I told auntie she told the nurse and she came in with a nappy. Even though I was ill I wasn't having that! Then another nurse came and switched off the pump and quick as a flash the first nurse lifted the lid, fastened the nappy on me and dropped the lid again. Putting her lips to my ear she whispered "fire away little man!" So I did and then the pump was started again and I felt really good.

When it was getting dark the doctor came back again. He told me they were going to take me out of the iron lung so that I could have a sleep. He opened his hand and showed me two little pills.

"These are called ephedrine," he said. "We've got them specially from China. As soon as you're out of the lung I want you to take them. When you do that those tubes will start to relax and you'll be able to breath more easily. They will make you feel a bit dreamy but don't let that bother you."

Soon it was done. As I fell into the cool sheets I really felt good. But after a while the wheezing feeling started again and I started to feel panicky. The nurse sat beside me and talked about not letting it worry me. She had a kind voice. And it was nice and soft. And then the dreamy feeling started and although I didn't go to sleep I felt drowsy and stopped worrying.

When it was really dark I fell asleep. But it wasn't for long. As soon as I started dreaming the terrifying pictures started again. Then I started gasping and choking and they came and put me back in my 'coffin'. I calmed down when it was getting light and was put back in the bed again.

It continued like that for some days. I would doze off. I'd wake up to find Auntie Mary sitting there. Then off I would go again. And then the choking and being carried to my 'coffin.' Then Auntie Mary would be gone for a while.

One day – when, I don't know because I'd lost all track of time – the door opened and a man came in. He wasn't wearing a white coat so I knew he wasn't a doctor. Then I looked more closely and saw it was Uncle Bill! Coming over to my bed he grabbed my hand.

"Don't get excited, Neil. Stay calm. No fuss!" Sitting down he pulled out a packet wrapped in brown paper and laid it on my locker. "Look at that after I've gone."

"Who's it from?"

"Your Mummy."

"Oh ..." I folded my arms and lay back in my pillow.

"She's been very poorly."

I didn't say anything.

"She's been having a sister for you."

"Oh ..." That didn't make me any happier as I thought I had too many brothers and sisters already.

"You're angry with her aren't you?"

"No, I don't know. Anyway, how did you get here?" I was really happy to see him and I didn't want to talk about anything else. "And where's your uniform. Did they sack you?"

"If I had my uniform on the Guards would be taking me off to prison camp. They'd have to intern me as Ireland is neutral."

Then he explained. When Mum heard I was ill she had rung him and asked if he could go and see me. He had contacted his Air Commodore who had given him a 72-hour pass. As the Air Force would not be able to help him, his boss had arranged for a friend to lend him his private Tiger Moth which was in Wales. He had then been authorized to make a 'training' flight on the Group's Dakota to Wales and off he went.

When he landed near Holyhead the Tiger Moth was fuelled up and ready to go. With permission from the Irish Air Corps he had crossed the sea and guided by one of their pilots who met him on the Irish coast, he had landed just outside Cork.

My eyes filled with tears as he told me the story. That a Squadron Leader, a Squadron Leader with a Distinguished Flying Cross could go to all that trouble for me, made me feel really happy.

I soon forgave Mum and felt sad I had been angry with her. While Uncle Bill was there I had to have another session in my iron lung and he helped the nurse carry me across. Then he sat at my head and chatted away until I nearly forgot about the pain of the sucking pump.

At about four o'clock he looked at his watch and stood up. He had to be back in England before it got dark. Tiger Moths had no night-flying equipment and crossing the Welsh coast in the wrong place would put him at risk from ack-ack batteries. With the help of the nurse he lifted me back to bed and then, with a last wave from the door, he was gone.

Opening the little parcel he had left I found a photo in a gilt frame. In it, Mum and Dad and two kids, Paddy and David were waving from the front drive of home. Bursting into tears I slid it under my pillow and fell asleep holding it tight.

Next day a friar came onto the ward. He was tall with ginger hair. He had a long brown cassock fastened round the waist with a thick cord from which a silver crucifix hung. The nurse explained he was a Franciscan and that as they were specially good with children in hospital the priests from the Cathedral said we should make them welcome.

After going round the ward he came over, shook my hand and introduced himself as Brother James. He was very soft-spoken. His eyes were wide and looked straight into mine. Deep down I knew he was the person I was looking for. After Uncle Bill left I did a lot of thinking. I realized how silly I had been, and selfish, thinking only of myself. A lot like Clare but it wasn't bags and dresses I wanted. I wanted to be awkward.

Why, I didn't know. But when I was and I was upsetting people it made me feel important. Auntie Mary had been with me day after day. Why? I reckoned it was because she was not being selfish. I also remembered my First Communion the year before and how terrified I'd been about committing sin. Now the chickens were coming home to roost.

"Can you give me confession, Father?" I didn't have to think about it. It came straight out.

He went and fetched a screen and put it behind his seat. Then he took his sash out and kissed it. "Go on then, Niall."

Then I started to cry. He didn't ask what the matter was or anything. He just sat and waited. After a while I calmed down.

"I burned Grant's down," I blurted.

"Do you want to tell me about it?"

He didn't look shocked or anything like that. In fact he didn't look anything. So I told him. After I had finished he sat quiet until he was sure that was it.

"Stink bombs?"

I nodded. "That's what he said."

"Stink bombs are no great sin, Niall. Do you think Finnegan was lying?"

I blew my nose. "I'm sure of it."

"Did you think he was lying when he took you in the store?"

"I don't know."

"Are you going to tell the *Gardaí*?"

"Do I have to?" I asked.

"What good do you think it would it do?"

I shrugged. "Make me feel better?"

"That's not a very good reason is it?" Brother James sat quiet for a while.

"Well?"

"Well what, Father?"

"You're going to cause a lot of upset to your Aunt and your Mam and Dad by trying to make

151

yourself feel better. Maybe that's selfish. Look," he leaned forward, "you don't know for certain those bombs were the cause of the fire. They might have been. They possibly were. But, you didn't do it with malice aforesight as the *Gardai* would say. You didn't intend it to happen. Maybe your friend did. But that's his affair isn't it? Let him sort that out with God."

He raised his hand and started "*absolvo te ...*"

Then he said, "say three rosaries. One for Finnegan, one for your Auntie Mary and one for all the staff at Grant's who have lost their jobs. Did you think of them?"

"No Father."

"Then do."

He put his hand on my head.

"It's gone now. Don't trouble yourself any more. Jesus has taken the blame on his shoulders. And they're more than strong enough to bear it."

I stayed in the hospital until late summer and when they had weaned me off the ephedrine pills and ensured I could cope, I was sent off to convalesce. They told me I'd be fine. I knew I would be. After my meeting with Father James the nightmares went and I slept well.

Uncle Tom, accompanied by Auntie Mary collected me from the hospital and we went on a long drive to Clifden, a place far out west where, so they say, they are nearer to America than any other town. As we went through West Galway, Auntie Mary pointed out Pearce's cottage, a little stone place in a wilderness of bogs and heather. Little streams and lakes dotted the landscape. The roads were windy. It seemed to me it would be an awful bleak place in winter.

I was to go to school in the town for a while. Every day I would leave the convalescent home with two other 'refugees' from Cork and we would trail along to school battling the winds blowing across the Atlantic. It seemed very healthy being away from the hustle of town and the smoke and I felt the strength pouring back into me.

My illness had been frightening and drained my confidence but that was now returning and I felt ready for anything. Uncle Tom fetched me home for Christmas. After the holiday I was to go back to Christians. I looked forward to it. The New Year went well. There was no snow and although I had a supply of ephedrine I didn't need it.

But things stopped going well in early March. Suddenly, without looking for it, the past was back to haunt me. Coming home from school, passing the hat factory by Shandon, I saw Finnegan walking towards me. Ducking into a doorway I held my breath.

"Not so fast, young man." A large hand grabbed my collar and pulled me out. "We've got some unfinished business ..."

As he pushed his face up to mine I could smell the whisky. He wasn't looking well. His eyes were bloodshot and he had a twitch running up from his jaw.

I wriggled. "Let me go I'm off home."

"Home!" he mocked. "And where's that now?"

"Nicholas Well Lane."

"No it's not. It's certainly not, Niall Murphy. I've been there looking for you for months now. Where have you been?"

"I've been ill."

"Ill, is it?" Walking me down the street he stepped into a pub taking me with him. "Sit down," he ordered, "and stay sitting."

He returned from the bar with two glasses, one of which he put in front of me. "Once you're in, there's no way out." His eyes narrowed to slits. "No scrimshankers, no going back, Niall." He took a swig from his glass. "Since you've been 'ill', we've had nothing from the docks. And we're waiting on information. It matters."

"I have started," I told him truthfully.

Clare had seen to that. She was sympathetic when I was ill. Well, not really sympathetic, perhaps unwillingly understanding. But now I was hale and hearty again she was back looking for her pound of flesh. So I'd started filling in my book and the mission was doing a roaring trade. The sisters had been really kind and told me not to overdo things. But they didn't know the pressure I was under.

The Grant's business was in the past. To me, that is, but whether the *Gardai* would see it in the same light as Father James, I doubted. So it was back to watching my Ps and Qs with Clare.

"I've got some names already. The book should be full by the end of the week."

"Good man!" Finnegan patted my shoulder,

smiling now. "And I do know you've been away sick because I made enquiries. But now I can see you're well again, well enough for a big job. That's good because you're just the man for it."

"What is it?"

He lowered his voice. "I'll tell you about it later. But for now you'll be coming out with me on a journey. Into West Cork."

"How will we get out there?"

"Motor bike. My bike. It's a runner, a real runner. We'll be far and back in a day."

"It'll have to be a Sunday. Auntie would catch on if it was a school day."

"So Sunday it is. Not this one but next. Okay?"

"Where will you pick me up."

"Cattle market, top of the cattle market, early. You can tell them it's a school Mass thing so they'll not be dragging you off to Saint Mary's."

"I'll be there," I said.

Here I go again, I thought. Leaving the pub I trudged home. I didn't really want to go but I liked the thought of a long bike ride. Besides, I had seen the bulge in his jacket as he went to the bar. He still had his gun with him.

Chapter Nine

Finnegan was waiting for me the next Sunday, sitting on a big Triumph. His head was wrapped in a scarf. He had one for me as well and after wrapping up we were off, down past Mardyke onto the Western Road and out into the country. I clasped his waist, hanging on like grim death as we roared along. The roads were clear as it was a Sunday and I could read around his shoulder we were doing seventy miles an hour, sometimes eighty. Bejesus, it felt good!

They were just leaving Mass at Clonakilty as we went through. Slowing to weave through the crowds I could look around. The main street was made up of little whitewashed cottages with half-doors opening onto the pavement. Pigs and dogs wandered around as if they had no owners and kids were everywhere, half of them without shoes, the cost of which I guessed was being spent in Dennis Fahy's. This was the long, low pub from which came the clouds of turf and tobacco smoke that hung like mist along the street. Squads of chickens and strutting cocks scratched at tufts of grass for their dinner. Shawlies sat on chairs brought out from their houses, watching the world and us, go by.

Beyond the village were the emerald fields dotted

with turf stacks and more pigs snouting and grunting. Then, as we passed a ruined farmhouse, Finnegan without a word of warning, swung through its gate and pulled up against the whitewashed wall of a crumbling privy. He turned the engine off, pulled the gun from his pocket and raced around the house, crouching, to where he could look back down the road. I crouched down too but apart from shrieking seagulls there was nothing, no one. Absolutely nothing.

After a few minutes he grunted "we're alright." Sliding the gun back inside his coat he walked back to the bike. "We're alright. We've lost them."

"Lost who?"

"Oh, they've been following us. You can be sure of that. But we've foxed them." Sitting on the wall he took out his flask and took a deep swig. "Yes. We've foxed them."

His eyes scanned the fields all round us. "The green of them is heartbreaking, isn't it Neil? Them and the blue sky. It's worth dying for. Don't you think so?"

For a few moments he was lost in thought.

"And a lot did die, Neil. The Tans rampaged round the countryside in their Crossley lorries but the lads were getting smart."

He pointed to where the road climbed wearily up a hill. "See there. They were waiting for them. Parked an old cart across the road, just on the bend, they did. The Tans didn't stand a chance. You could hear the shooting from the village. Everyone went into their houses and barred the doors. But it didn't save them. Next day four lorries of Tans and Auxiliaries drove in from Cork. Burnt some of the houses."

"Did you see it?"

"I did. I was there. They shot my Dad. Had to run the farm myself after that." He sighed deeply. "They pushed my Mammy down the stairs. Broke her back."

He stood up and walked back to the bike. "Every dog has its day, Neil. And I'm doing the barking now. Come on."

Happy now we were not being followed he travelled at a more leisurely pace, heading towards the sea where I could see the horizon clear as a drawn line. After a while the surface changed into mud track and then to grass along the cliff tops. Cutting the engine he pushed the bike into undergrowth and stood gazing over the water.

"Over there, just off Kinsale," he pointed, "that's where the Lucy went down. The Lusitania. Sunk in fifteen minutes, she did. Over a thousand drowned. They stood on the cliffs and watched her go down. Not a boat launched to help. Had to wait for the Royal fecking Navy to come from Cork. She was carrying armaments. The Germans knew that so they had no pity. But we were having nothing to do with it either. Callous? Maybe we were but the Brits were more so."

He paused. "Then, a year later they shot all those lads, Pearce and the rest at Kilmainham Prison. No, Neil, the Brits will never get a welcome here. Any enemy of England is a friend of ours. And now I'm taking you to see some of those friends."

Pulling his motorbike back out of the bushes we jumped on and headed west. Killarney was silent as we blasted through it into raw country. Mile after mile with bends in the road where we nearly touched the ground.

As we skirted a headland, Finnegan pointed west to a little cove nestled between cliffs. It had turned into a lovely day. The sea was a really deep blue and apart from a thin line of surf it was difficult now to see where the water ended and the sky started.

"See there. See, under the cliffs?" he pointed.

I rubbed my eyes. Driving through fields and over grass had given me a bit of hay fever. At first all I could see was a grey line in the water, like a pier with waves washing against it. Half-way along it was a dirty grey tower with poles sticking up from it and a gun. The waves struck it and plumes of water shot into the air and when the foaming water retreated I saw the whole structure.

"It's a U-boat!" I gasped. It looked evil, lying there low in the water, like a monster waiting for its prey.

"It's a U-boat alright. And it's here to meet us. We're going to help the Germans destroy the British Empire, you and me." He spoke with a softness I found frightening. "The English boil that needs lancing. And, down there is the knife that will help us do it. Come on now."

From the top of the cliff we started down a narrow path to the beach. I was a bit frightened now and thought about Uncle Bill and Father James. Auntie Mary wouldn't like me being involved in all

160

this either. But Clare would think it was good *craic* if there was money in it. And Finnegan had promised it would be good money. And then I remembered the last 'big job' was to be good money. "Live like a lord", he said. All I got out of that was nearly dying and spending half a year in a hospital and convalescent home.

The drop from the cliff edge had started off frightening but the path was okay and in a few minutes we were ankle deep in sand. The beach was empty but we could hear shouting and laughing from the other side of a ridge of craggy rock running down from the cliff and out to sea.

I followed Finnegan to where the ridge met the waves and picked my way over seaweed and little pools. On the other side was a bigger beach and only a few yards offshore below the far cliff of the cove was the U-boat moving gently up and down.

An area of sand had been cleared and marked out with lines of seaweed. There must have been twenty people on the beach. A number of men in shorts or uniform trousers with braces were waving hurley sticks chasing a small ball, trying to get it into a goal knocked up from driftwood. The beach was like the Roman amphitheatres you see in pictures and the shouting and cheering echoed off the high cliff. On the far side of the pitch was a gaggle of girls, their dresses flapping in a stiff breeze, talking to another group of men. Several others were standing in a circle round the only man wearing a cap.

Finnegan introduced me to *Der Alte*, the "Old Man", as the captain was addressed. Although he seemed to be enjoying himself his face looked tired and pale. He gave me mock salute, took the pipe out of his mouth and grunted "hello, young feller."

At that moment the wind whistled up the beach throwing eddies of sand high into the air in little fountains. The girls screamed and were brushing it away from their faces and out of their hair. Their skirts lifting had shown some lovely legs.

"A fine sight for a weary sailor!" *Der Alte* grinned at the both of us.

Finnegan shaded his eyes as he looked towards the horizon. "Why aren't they swimming, Captain? The water's lovely. Freshen them up. Nearly as good as a bath!"

"Indeed, Mister Finnegan. It is two months since they had a good bath and could be two more. But if a Catalina or a Sunderland appears we are in trouble."

"The Brits wouldn't dare," Finnegan pronounced.

Der Alte raised his eyebrows. "We are protected by the cliff but they do not give up easily. They could not get a torpedo in the cove but would *strafe* and apologise to your government later. We stay close to *das boot*, I think."

He brushed the sand film off his face and his cap and looked at me, grinning. "Now, my friends we will go aboard. Is that alright?"

"Thank you, Sir! I would really like to see inside!"

I got my shoes and socks wet stepping into a little dinghy that had been pulled half out of the water. Two of the crew pushed it back until it floated. It only took a minute for two other crewmen to row us out which was good because I started to feel sick from the bobbing about.

The gun was big when you got close up. An 88 millimetre *schiffskanone* with a range of over twelve kilometres, my notes said. Cousin Billy had helped me look up information on it after seeing one on the way over to Dublin. It was pointing in our direction but to the top of the cliff. Two other sailors on the gun platform at the rear of the conning tower were staring seaward. One of them came down some iron rung steps and held the rope from the dingy. There was no saluting or anything like that. In fact they looked quite untidy.

The captain said something in German and received the clipped reply, *"ja, Herr Alte!"*

The torpedo loading door in the middle of the deck was open and I was helped down. As soon as we were out of the fresh sea breeze a horrible smell of lavatories, cabbage, sweat and diesel oil caused me almost to gag.

"Ha," the captain grinned, "you do not like the smell of our submarine! Not exactly *Eau de Cologne*, eh?"

"How in the name of God do you put up with it?" Finnegan wrinkled his nose. "I'd be sick."

"You get used to it. You don't notice it quickly. Now, careful with your heads as we go through."

Shepherding us to a control room which had as many pipes and tubes around it as the belly of a cow, *Der Alte* waved us into a compartment that looked and smelt like a toilet. "Squeeze around the table, please."

Going to a little safe on the wall, he fiddled with the lock and pulled out an envelope. He took a photograph from the envelope and put it on the table. "The SS Irish Oak, my friends. Do you recognise her?"

Finnegan grunted. I shook my head. It could have been any of them in Cork harbour. A six-thousand tonner, single piper. Irish flags showed stem and stern and EIRE was painted in white on its side under the bridge.

"Yes, they are all similar, these coasters. But this one," he banged his fist on the table sending a half-full mug of cold coffee to the floor, "this one is a spy ship!"

"Spy ship!" Finnegan echoed, putting his finger on the photograph.

"Indeed, Mister Finnegan. She claims neutrality with her markings. She is safe out of convoy, we leave them alone. But very strange she still travels in convoy. Fifty kilometres ahead, maybe, or fifty astern. So what is she doing?"

"She's spying, Captain!" Finnegan said, as though a light had switched on. "She's spying on your U-boats!"

"Indeed she is, *Herr* Finnegan. We have picked up her signals to sister ships in the convoy. And, what do you know, a corvette, or if we are very unlucky, a destroyer heads for us. We are losing many submarines. Dönitz is particularly tired of fake Irish ships. This ship we want quickly now. She is not neutral. She is as much the enemy as the Royal Navy."

He pulled a packet of cigarettes from his pocket, handed one to Finnegan and lit them both. Finnegan pulled out his hanky and wiped his brow.

"This is big stuff, Captain. Being involved with this sort of thing we could be hanged. It's classed as murder."

The captain turned to me. "Young Niall. You are good at getting information, I hear. What do you think?"

I looked at Finnegan and he nodded back.

"If *Herr*, er, Mister Finnegan goes along with it, I'll go along with it."

Finnegan took a deep drag of the cigarette, lifted his head and blew three smoke rings which, in the confined air of the submarine hovered gently over us. Then he lifted his hand and flicked them away.

"We'll do it," he said with an evil grin on his face. "Anything to get those feckin' Brits by the balls. We'll do it."

"*Das ist gut*, very good." *Der Alte* rose slowly, took something else from the safe and handed it to Finnegan. "The Irish Oak is on the American side at the moment. As soon as you can please, find which port she is leaving or which one arriving. Dates also."

My jaw dropped as Finnegan unwrapped the brown paper packet and flicked carefully through banknotes with a dark blue border. I hadn't seen a ten pound note before. I'd never seen a wad either.

Der Alte leaned back in his chair and dragged on the cigarette. "As soon as you can, please, *herren*. This time we sink her."

Chapter Ten

Leaving Bantry behind us, we skimmed over the hills and just before Clonakilty, Finnegan swung onto a second class road signed to Dunmanway. At first I thought he might be trying to avoid pursuers again but no, for the moment, that worry had left him. His meeting with *Der Alte* had revitalized him and as we roared round the sharp bends brushing hedges I heard him humming. In fact the more cheerful he became the faster we went and the tighter I hung on. A picture of us shooting through the hedge after hitting something, anything, or even nothing more than a strong breeze, swept through my head.

In the end, however, he slowed down, the engine faded and we rolled onto the grass in the middle of nowhere. Jumping off, Finnegan raised his hands high over his head and after dancing around a bit like a maniac pulled out his gun and loosed two shots into the road.

"This is where it happened Niall! Right here. This is where we saw the Brits off!"

He fired another shot. Then retrieving his faithful companion from inside his jacket he pulled the cork and took a long swig.

"Did you never hear of Kilmichael? This is the

place where we saw them off. Defeated the British Empire. Yes!" He got down to his knees and jabbed his finger at the road. "On this very spot. We shot them all, Tom Barry's lads. T'was a miserable Sunday morning. Along they came in their Crossleys. Tom walks up and drops a grenade on the lead driver's lap. Then it all started. We killed seventeen of them. All Auxiliaries. Worse than the Tans. One of them ran into that bog there. He splashed deeper until he was up to his knees. Then he couldn't move. So he tried to lie still over the turf. Tom sent me after him. Whimpering he was with his hands over his face, pleading. I put a bullet in him, though. Shut him up." His eyes were shining. "Shut him to feck up."

The countryside around the ambush site was empty of life. No cows, no sheep, no birds, no colour as if it was haunted and people should stay away. The excitement of the submarine and the captain and the hurley-playing sailors had gone. I felt sick, just like when that dog had been run over at home. The whining. A whining dog and a whining soldier. I could see it all, hear the shooting. Sitting down on the wet grass I leaned over and vomited.

Finnegan patted me on the shoulder. "Never mind. I'll make a soldier of you yet, Niall. A soldier for Ireland."

He pushed his bike off its stand and jumped on the starter. I climbed on and put my arms round his waist and off we went again with him singing his head off. All the way to Cork he sang, until he dropped me near the harbour. I didn't really feel like doing anything there but didn't want to go home either. Anyway, I had an idea.

Fog had dissolved everything into a grey. As I trudged down Glanmire Road I could see its fingers crawling up and over the station, mixing with the brown turf smoke from the trains. It wafted around as it met the soft breeze coming down Wellington Road, writhing as if it was trapped and wanting to get away, like the soldier who had run into the bog. I hated whining. Then I thought, maybe Finnegan had enjoyed the man's whining before he shot him? I could imagine it. If he was tanked up and had that look in his eyes I had seen, I would bet he had enjoyed it.

Walking along the quay there, two figures emerged from the gloom. They stood for a few seconds looking at me. One switched a torch on in my face. It was the *Gardai*.

"I'm John Twomey," the man said, "and beside me is *Banngarda* Aileen Riley. And now who might you be? You're not fishing now, are you, at this time of night?"

My heart was beating fast. "Niall Murphy, Sir."

The lady *Garda* rubbed her hands down my clothes. Thrusting her hand into my left pocket she let out an "Oh, my God!" and pulled out two cartridge cases. They were from Finnegan's gun, ejected onto the road after his wild moment at Kilmichael. I had picked them up to sell on at school. Anyone with a bit of experience could make grand little lighters from them and they were worth tuppence each.

"Look at these, John." The *Banngarda* held them up for inspection.

The *Garda* sniffed them. "Recently fired." He scanned my face again with his torch.

"So where did you get these from, now?"

"Collins Barracks, Sir." My mind went into overdrive. "I'm from Christians and they let us go up the hill to their rugby field."

"You've not being playing rugby today. You're too clean for that."

"My friends were playing so I went to watch. The field is by the shooting place. I picked these up on the way out."

He looked at me for a moment. "Where do you live?"

"Off Blarney Street, Sir."

"Well, get off back to Blarney Street. It's no place for a lad like you down here. You could be in the water before you know where you are."

"Yes, Sir." Turning round I started off only to be halted by the woman calling. "Yes, Miss?"

"You're English?"

"An evacuee, Miss. I'm from Sheffield."

Her voice softened. "Is your Mammy with you?"

"No, Miss. I'm with my Auntie."

"Ah sure, God love you! Get off home now. Don't come down here again." With that the two turned away and faded into the gloom.

Sister Ann opened the door when I arrived at the Mission.

"Come in, Niall." Grabbing my arm she pulled me through and closed the door. "You're alone?"

"The *Gardai* stopped me at the docks."

"What for?" I detected a note of anxiety in her voice.

"The fog. They're watching out." I followed her into the room. "Nothing to worry about. Just a few silly questions. Told me to go home before I fell in the water."

The place was surprisingly busy. I thought the fog would have kept everyone aboard their ships. But somehow they'd made it out. The Mission seemed to draw them.

Putting a glass of lemonade in front of me, Sister Ann slumped into a chair. "Have you any news then, Niall?"

"I've been out west today. Had a good time. Went out past Bantry." I looked around the room. There was a clutch of bottles on the table and several sailors playing cards. Most of them were talking in undertones and I couldn't tell what they were on about.

Sitting quietly I supped my lemonade. Then I crossed the room, sat beside them and murmured, "I met a lady whose husband is on the Irish Oak. She hadn't heard from him. She seemed worried. She didn't know when he would be home ..."

A man in a grubby peaked cap stubbed his cigarette out in the overflowing ashtray. "The Oak? Just set off, someone mentioned on the ship-to-shore. Arrives Dublin on the 25th. Aye, the 25th." He winked. "Her bed will be aired well enough by then." He gave a snort and the others joined in.

"There now!" Ann stood up and looked around.

"I think the chapel is free now. Do any of you want confession?"

Without a word, a young sailor with a thick donkey jacket put his cards down on the table and left the room. As his booted feet clumped up the stairs Ann pulled a pound from her pocket and nodded towards the hall door. "Don't want to be spoiling their card game Niall, do we?" she whispered, slipping the note into my hand. "Back tomorrow, then?"

"Tomorrow," I said, stuffing the money into my pocket.

Slipping into the 'phone box on Shandon Street, I found the pennies Finnegan had given me and dialed his number. A breathless female answered on the first ring. And without bothering with introductions and in case anyone was listening, I passed on the message that my cousin would be arriving from America at Dublin on the 25th. There was a brief "thank you" and the receiver was put down.

Then I trudged off home working out my excuse for being so late. I wasn't worried though. I knew that anything I said would be good enough. Auntie Mary trusted me and although I felt guilty about abusing that trust my worries about Clare were stronger. She'd got me in a grip. But I was also elated at being so helpful. It was just too easy.

Next day I went to school as normal but at dinnertime I hiked up to St. Angela's where Jean was. After persuading a nun to let her out into the garden, we spent a half-hour together talking about this and that. But not about what Clare was always going on about. Actually, everything was going well again. Business boomed during the week at the docks and Clare couldn't be happier.

Everything changed, however, the following Saturday morning. As I was having my breakfast, Clare and her mother were going on about Clare's plans for staying with her friend for the weekend. We always had Radio Éireann on first thing. You didn't really listen, it was just background. You heard nothing until something came up that was like a tap on the head. In this instance, it was the phrase 'Irish Oak'. Jumping up I went into the sitting room and turned the radio up.

A few moments later, the news, a real headline-maker was repeated. In a sonorous voice the announcer told that the Irish Oak, a freighter of 6,000 tons had been torpedoed on its way to the shores of Ireland. The ship had radioed for help. No more information was known about the fate of the ship or its crew. That was all the announcer said.

It was like someone had dropped a huge weight on me. My spine went all funny and I had a scratchy feeling over the top of my head. Then I felt dizzy. The living room door opened wide and I saw Clare looking at me quizzically.

"You're looking pale. Are you ill?" Before I could reply she had called, "Mammy, Niall is looking poorly."

"I'm not ill. It's just ..."

"Just what? Is it that asthma again?" Auntie Mary looked worried. She put her hand on my forehead.

"You do feel hot."

Panic started to well over me. My head was completely taken up with a huge picture, like a film running, of a ship sinking. I could see waves washing over the bows chasing men around the deck as they frantically lowered lifeboats. The year before I had read about the Irish Pine, Oak's sister ship. She had sunk within minutes of being torpedoed. Everyone had drowned. Now it was the Oak and it was my doing. Pushing past Clare and her Mammy I raced down the path, down to the 'phone box at the bottom of Blarney Street. It was empty and slotting in pennies, I dialled Finnegan's number.

"It's sunk. They've sunk it," I blurted out to the voice that answered, the woman again.

"Wait. I'll fetch himself." The receiver went down and after a few seconds Finnegan came on.

"Now, what's this all about?"

"The Irish Oak. It's been torpedoed," I blurted out sobbing now. There was a pause before he answered in a matter-of-fact tone,

"So I heard on the news. And what's that to do with us, now?"

"Everything. It's got everything to do with us," I said, finally bursting into tears.

"Now calm yourself, for God's sake!" Finnegan responded, his patience was straining.

"I'm going to the *Gardai*," I sobbed.

"Oh no you won't ..."

"I am," I wailed. And out of the corner of my eye I saw several people looking on, concerned. While I had been blurting out our secrets, a queue had formed outside the box and the man at its head was now tapping on the door.

"I've got to go," I said, calming suddenly.

"Wait ..." Finnegan was anxious now. "I'll come across. You can tell me all about it at the Mercy Hospital. I'll park up by Granville Street. And remember, I owe you some money ..."

Wiping my eyes on my sleeve I left the box. Everyone in the queue must have thought I'd had bad news so no-one said anything. Going down Blarney Street I crossed North Gate Bridge and turning right, followed the river.

Finnegan was waiting there, not at Granville Street. His face was covered with a scarf. His jacket was belted so tight I could make out the shape of his pistol in his right-hand pocket.

"Get on." He nodded towards his pillion.

"I've got to get back, we're going out."

"Get on ..." his hand strayed towards his pocket, "... get on the fecking bike. What do you think you're doing, compromising me over the fecking telephone?"

I didn't know what he meant but instinct kicked in. The tone of his voice had changed. I made my mind up. The man was a killer. I wasn't imagining it. He'd told me himself and he'd enjoyed telling me. It wasn't something he was ashamed of. If I had killed someone like that injured soldier, no matter who he was, I would have felt bad about it. I wasn't getting on his bike.

Pulling out his flask he took a deep swig. It was early in the morning and he was on the booze. Even

Uncle Tom didn't start until dinnertime. The admiration I had for Finnegan suddenly faded as the realization struck me he was no good. All his talk of Ireland was moonshine. He was just out for himself.

"That captain gave you money. A wad. How much was in it?"

"Never you bloody mind about that." Starting his bike he inched slowly towards me. "Just get on the bike."

"No, you're drunk. You'll have an accident." I wasn't going to have anything to do with him any more. He made a grab for me. I kicked the front wheel hard. The handlebar turned and he wasn't quick enough to stop himself and the bike falling over. When he managed to get it off him, he stood up, holding his leg. Then he pulled the gun out of his pocket.

"I'll kill you, you little fecking traitor."

But he wasn't going to get the chance. I could run better than him in his heavy gear and dodgy leg and I took off down the road. There was a footbridge at the end with poles to stop traffic using it. I only had a hundred yards to go when I heard the bike start up. I could make it in ten seconds.

But the bike was faster than my opinion of my running and I was ten yards off the poles when he drew alongside. Pulling his gun out again he screamed at me to stop. But with only one hand driving and heavy with booze the bike wasn't having any of it. A big hole in the road sealed his fate as he tried to accelerate in front of me. The bike wobbled and with a sickening crack hit a tree on the pavement edge. The engine cut out and there was silence.

On reaching the safety of the little bollards I turned, breathing hard. Finnegan was still mounted but slumped forward against the tree. The front wheel had flown off and the trunk wedged between the front forks was holding the bike upright. He was sitting there like someone stupid staring, not at me but at the road, his head flopped sideways on his shoulder.

Then I saw fuel dripping. It had gathered in a little pool on the pavement and was trickling towards a drain. Then with a soft whooshing, it ignited. In a moment flames were licking all around his body. Then the heat ruptured the tank and the stuff flooded out and then I could hardly see him in the blaze.

Leaves on the tree started hissing and curling as the flames went higher. Some people gathered but couldn't get near the bike. By the time the fire engine arrived it was all over. Finnegan was black and the blaze had finished, apart from a few puffs of smoke from under his arms.

I walked off in a daze when I heard the clanging. Nobody was on the bridge so I pulled the gun out of my pocket. It had slid along the road after me when the bike struck the tree. I dropped it quietly into the river and set off towards the quay.

By the time I had reached the barracks at the Rock Steps I was shaking and couldn't stop crying. I couldn't get the picture of Finnegan, his face against the tree and the roaring flames and the smell, out of my head. He gave off a smell as he burned and that, mixed with petrol fumes and choking smoke filled my nose. Leaning against the wall I retched and watched the sick tumbling into the water. This was the end of it.

There was a little hatch on the passage wall of the barracks. After I had tapped it slid open and a sergeant with grey hair and a big red nose grunted. He was writing in a big ledger and didn't bother looking up.

"What is it?"

"I've been wicked." I hesitated but then repeated myself, blubbing.

"Confession's at Saint Mary's. Starts at lunchtime."

The sergeant raised his head. Behind him were two *gardai* holding mugs of tea, looking on inquisitively. A *banngarda* came in from a door at the back of the large office and hearing my sobs she also looked over the sergeant's shoulder.

"It's Niall, isn't it? Remember, the other night at the docks?"

"I've sunk a ship," was all I managed to say before a Niagara of tears flooded down my face. Coming out from the office, Aileen, I remembered, gave me a hanky and guided me into the barracks and into a little room.

Sitting me down she said, "now, you tell me all about it."

Chapter Eleven

There was a long corridor with a high roof and little arches strung along it and posh-looking columns like you see in some churches. It was painted cream and the carpet, which was pale green was so soft you couldn't hear people coming. It was like Cork library. Then a door opened, there was a buzz of conversation, the tingling of 'phone bells and then the door shut and silence reigned again.

"Don't worry," Aileen gave my hand a squeeze. "You're not going to be done away with."

She'd come all the way from Cork with me. She was my escort, as it was called. We'd left Cork station on the seven o'clock train. I had only a small bag of stuff. It contained everything I had, a few clothes, a toothbrush, the picture of Mum and Dad and an ivory statue of the Sacred Heart given to me for my first communion. They said it was ivory but a corner had been knocked off and I could see it was Plaster of Paris that had been covered with varnish.

I'd spent the night at Aileen's house. They had wanted to put me in the Boys' Home but they had no beds.

Being under arrest didn't worry me. I felt as if I'd been under arrest since beimg in Ireland. Not that they had been unkind to me. In fact they had all been lovely. It was me who had been unkind to them. But it wasn't home. My home was where Mum lived and Dad and Paddy and now, though I hadn't seen him as he arrived after I had left, a new brother, David.

Brother Maher had come to the Barracks to see me. It wasn't me he wanted to see really but to talk to them about me. But since he was there he came to talk to me as well. He wasn't cross but he sat there slowly shaking his head, looking sad. He didn't say much but we did a decade of the rosary. I didn't have one so he borrowed one from Aileen who was sitting in. Then he left and told me, "God bless you!"

Aileen said they had been on the 'phone to Dublin and we had to go up there tomorrow. There were some reports to be prepared and she wanted to know who, apart from the O'Reillys could tell them about me. Since arriving in Ireland I'd had a lot of attacks of asthma and seen a doctor on Wellington Hill who talked to me a lot. I couldn't remember his name but Auntie Mary would know it.

Then there was Sister Ann. I told Aileen about the work I had done for the mission and that they had paid me quite a lot of money which I had given to Clare for dresses. She didn't know anything about the mission by the station so I gave her the details. After that she went away and an hour later I heard Sister Ann come in. Aileen was with her and from what I could hear, things weren't very friendly between them. I waved to her when I went to the toilet. She was sitting in the cell area. She didn't wave back. I asked Aileen if I could see her before I went off to Dublin but she said no.

There was a *Garda* car waiting at Dublin station. It took us to this big place. There were lots of *Gardai* about with guns. When they saw Aileen's uniform they waved us through. Once we had stopped there was a young man waiting for us. He was very nice to Aileen but he didn't even look at me. Then there were stairs and more *Gardai*. But we had no problems.

Then there was a door. A big double door and a man standing outside it. He kept looking at us. Then another door opened and a lady came down. She nodded to the man outside the door. He came across and asked me to stand up. Then he ran his hands over me, legs, tummy and everything else. I felt like laughing.

The lady was doing the same to Aileen who looked surprised. I thought she was thinking that being a *banngarda* she could be trusted. The lady who was searching her must have felt that too because she whispered "Mister de Valera has a lot of enemies, as you know. So we have to be careful my dear." Then she nodded to the man who had gone back to standing by the door and he knocked on it and pushing it open, waved us to go in.

By this time my knees were shaking. Aileen had let go of my hand. As we stood there she gave a salute. And then a voice said "please sit down, Miss. Over there." And as she moved away I saw two large dark eyes looking very serious.

Well, if they hadn't crucified Jesus, left him to live

for a few more years then plastered his hair with Brylcreem, that was the man I was looking at. Uncle Tom called Mr. de Valera the "Devil of Ireland" and others did too. But he didn't look like that to me. He didn't look soft either. I thought he looked like the school teacher who dealt with Class Three at Christians. He seemed to have that knack of saying little but with a lot in it.

"So you're Neil Murphy?"

It wasn't really a question because he knew who I was. You wouldn't get kids running round the place, popping in here and there and him asking who they were. So I said nothing while he looked me over.

"*Cad is ainm duit?*"

"*Niall O'Murcadha is ainm dum.*"

"The accent is good. Very Cork. Now let me hear the Hail Mary."

"*So do beatha a Mhuire ata lan de ghrasta, ta Tiarna leat ...*"

He put his hand up. "Yes, very Cork indeed." He picked up a sheet of paper, looked it up and down and looked back at me. "Brother Maher says you won a prize for public speaking. What piece did you do?"

"Robert Emmet, Sir."

"His speech from the dock?"

"Yes, Sir."

"Let me hear the last paragraph."

"In Irish, Sir?"

"He spoke it in English. Do that."

I took a deep breath. It was so powerful a speech

I would never forget the last words of the hero as he went to be hanged.

"The grave opens to receive me and I sink into its bosom. I have but one request to make at my departure from this world. It is the charity of its silence. Let no man write my epitaph; for as no man who knows my motives dare now vindicate them, let not prejudice or ignorance asperse them. Let them and me rest in obscurity and peace; and my tomb remain uninscribed and my memory in oblivion until other times and other men can do justice to my character. When my country takes her place among the nations of the earth, then, and not till then let my epitaph be written. I have done ..."

I liked the sound of my own voice and as I had won the prize I knew others did to. Even though just a kid, I found this speech very sad and it could make me cry. But here, in this office, knowing the man I was addressing had been on an English execution list, I was quite overcome. Dev, his chin resting on his fingers, had tears trickling down his cheeks too. Taking out his hanky he blew his nose and then nodded.

"That's a good voice you have, Neil. And you sing too?"

"No," he held up his hand as I took a deep breath, "I'll take your word for it."

He sat brooding for a while and then he addressed Aileen. "What about this Finnegan, Miss?"

As she went to stand he motioned her to sit. "That's not his name, Sir."

"Were you on the investigation?"

"I was, Sir. With Sergeant Sullivan. We have no record of him."

"If it was an alias, you wouldn't would you?"

"You're correct, Sir. But he wasn't a ghost ..."

"Although he is now!"

"That's right, *Taoiseach*. He was known around the pubs. He had a nickname, 'Thirsty'."

Dev laughed. "For his drinking habits?"

"And his way of getting others to buy his round."

"Was he at Kilmichael?"

"Everyone in West Cork was at Kilmichael." She smiled, then blushed. "I'm sorry, Sir. But from what I hear, there are about two hundred claimants to the er, honour."

"Apart from Tom Barry."

"Sir?"

"All would-be heroes? But according to Neil's statement, Finnegan claimed he'd been shot in the head?"

She nodded. "The post mortem found a deep scar across the skull. But it hadn't penetrated the brain."

"Ah! it could have been from a hurley bat in a brawl or falling drunk on the pavement?"

"It could, Sir."

"And his pistol?"

"We searched the river, Sir, but found nothing. The current's strong there. Could have been washed into the docks. But we found live bullets in his pocket. Four fifty-fives. They matched the cartridge cases Niall had picked up."

"A Webley. Pinched from the British?"

"Recovered from a British Officer's body at Kilmichael, I would think."

He nodded. "Very likely."

Turning to his secretary who was taking notes he held out his hand and a buff-coloured file was passed over.

"And the mission. Go on Neil, tell me about it."

I shrugged. "Sister Ann came up to me on the docks and asked me to take any sailors to the mission. She said there would be some drink and food for them. And friendly company."

"Friendly company?"

"Yes, Sir. They said they had a little chapel upstairs and they used to take them there to pray. And confession if they wanted it."

"Can I explain, Sir?" Aileen interrupted. "These 'sisters' used to work the quays but we put extra patrols on to clear them out. Some ended up in court."

The *Taoiseach* shook his head slowly, looking at Neil. "So they used you as their agent?"

"No one would suspect a little boy." Aileen answered again for me, speaking softly.

"So now?"

"We've shut them down, Sir. They're like mushrooms though. They'll be back."

"And they paid you?"

"Half a crown, Sir."

Aileen shifted in her seat. "He's a bit naïve, Sir. He genuinely didn't catch on."

"This submarine. How did that happen?" He was

looking at Aileen now as she was explaining things.

"There are a lot of men leaning on each other in Cork. German agents, *Abwehr* they call them. Old IRA, would-be IRA. All part of so-called Operation Shamrock. Willing to get involved in all sorts of tricks for a drink and for glory. There's a lot of fantasy in it. But there's an element of reality in it as well. They're like blindfolded fools in a dark room. Eejits, Sir."

"And they sucked Neil into the whole thing?"

"Yes, Sir. Submarines do come in to the southwest. The locals don't mind them. And the girls are head-over-heels."

Dev spoke softly but seriously. "We know about the signals from down there. The British have got the situation under control."

Then he looked at me. "How did you find out about the Irish Oak?"

"At the mission, Sir."

"And didn't it strike you that what you were doing was wicked? That men could be killed?"

I lowered my head as tears trickled down my cheeks.

"If you had been grown-up you could have been in great trouble for what you did."

"I'm sorry, Sir. So sorry."

He looked at the papers in front of him again in silence. "Doctor McCarthy says in his report that your asthma attacks started after arriving in Cork. They never happened in England?"

I looked at him dumbly.

"The report says it could be psychosomatic. Do

186

you know what that means?"

I shook my head slowly.

"It means that you are missing your Mam. How long is it since you've seen her?"

"Four years."

"And that's why you are having the attacks. What do you think of that?"

"Michael, my brother, was very unhappy and they sent him back to England. But I liked it here."

"Alright. Let's leave it there. Now," he continued softly but looking at me very seriously, "I'm not going to go over all your offences again. I am satisfied you now realize the wrong things you've done. But what am I going to do? You have broken a long list of Irish laws. I am responsible for ensuring that laws are kept. And how am I going to do that?"

He raised his eyebrows. "Well?"

I shuffled uncomfortably. I didn't know what he wanted me to say so I said nothing.

"Right then. I've made up my mind. And now it's necessary for you to listen very carefully. As you know, Ireland is not at war. But we do have a *Re na Prainna.*"

"You understand that?"

"No, Sir."

"It's what we call a State of Emergency. This is because of the fighting around us. We consider ourselves to be at risk. And because of this the *Dáil* has passed what's called the Emergency Powers Act. This gives me very great powers. I can do almost anything I want without asking anyone. I couldn't rob a bank but if Ireland needed it, I could order any bank to hand over to the government as much money as we felt we needed. You're looking puzzled?"

"Well, yes, Sir. But I haven't done anything with banks."

"I know that, Neil. It is just an illustration." He opened a drawer and pulled out a document which the secretary brought over to me. "This is a deportation order. Because you are English I can order you to leave the country of Ireland. And I don't have to give anyone, judges or anyone else, a reason. And I can do it even though you are still only nine years old, almost ten. So that's what I'm going to do. Send you back to England. All the things you have done wrong are being held on a file. No action will be taken on them by the courts. And after ten years, this file will be destroyed and that will be an end to it."

He looked at Aileen. "I understand he's going tomorrow?"

"A cousin is taking him, Sir. From Cork station to Sheffield. She has found work in England."

"Her name is?"

"Dillon, Sir. Miss Dillon, eldest daughter of Niall's Aunt Kate."

"Right, now.' He handed an envelope to Aileen. "This is a personal note to your Superintendant. I want it hand-delivered. It orders and authorizes him to get rid permanently of all the papers to do with this matter. I don't want to be seeing it all in the Cork Examiner in a few days' time. Secrecy is of the

188

essence." He looked at her. "Who does know anything about it? Has it been going the rounds of Cork?"

"Not at all, Sir. Apart from Mister and Missers O'Reilly and Brother Maher and the doctor it's been completely confidential."

"Good," he nodded. "And we'll keep it that way."

Standing up he pressed a bell and the doorman came in. "They are ready."

He turned to me again. "That's it, Neil. The order bans you from coming back to Ireland again for ten years. With any luck the war should be over by then and we'll be happy to see you back. But if you try to return in under ten years we'll have to arrest you and open that file." He wagged his finger. "Remember that now!"

He patted my shoulder. "Go back to your Mammy now. God bless!"

As we walked back down the corridor I took a deep breath. So that was it. Kicked out. Back to the bombs. And to Mum and Dad who may not be very happy to see me. But it hadn't been too frightening an experience. Dev looked a tough guy and I was worried it could have been Borstal. So now I felt great.

"I'm going home!"

"You are!" Aileen gave me a squeeze. "And you're a lucky lad. A very lucky lad!"

It was stormy the next day. The wind was driving the sea into patterns of peaks and troughs and as the bow dipped, spray foamed up and ran along the deck to run out again through the rails in tumbling waterfalls. I grabbed hold of the rails and had a last look back at the shrinking coastline of Ireland.

Leaving Cork had been sad. Auntie Mary had cried and kissed me and hugged me. Jean said I was lucky going home to see Mum and Dad and she would be all on her own and she cried. Uncle Tom was at the station as well but I don't think he cared. I wasn't bothered at seeing the last of him.

And Clare! She was furious. Her little money-making schemes were finished. Her dresses would soon be falling to rags. But I didn't care. I think I blamed her for what had happened. At any rate it stopped me from blaming myself.

Nobody would understand how she could get onto you unless it happened to them. How those eyes of hers could bore into you. And the way she was so horrible when I did something wrong.

But it didn't matter now. I thought when she was properly grown up she would lead someone a right merry dance and I thanked God it wouldn't be me. I was well out of it now.

Chapter Twelve

I had no idea what to expect back in England in the Summer of 1943 and I was quite shocked. Not at anything said to me like, why had I been sent home? No questions were asked and nothing was ever said, not a word. By the time the war was over I think my parents and Michael and my new brothers and sister, had other things to think about and it was all just forgotten.

I was shocked at the devastation. Coming back from Liverpool Docks, through Manchester to Sheffield was awesome. Whole areas had been flattened, with only the occasional pile of rubble reminding you what had been. Not the steelworks, though. When we reached Sheffield the gloom confirmed the bombing hadn't affected them. They were still pumping out their smoke.

The City Centre was gone. Navvies were still working lethargically recovering bricks, stones and baulks of wood from the ruins of more than two years before. They just seemed weary sitting round the little fires burning wood they could do nothing with, watching the thin grey smoke drift up and away as if glad to be out of it.

The Town Hall, standing proud over the deserted

streets had survived and still flaunted the naked statue of Vulcan, the God of metalworkers, atop its tower.

"Standing by the Town Hall,
looking at its clock,
while far up above, was
Vulcan and his cock ..."

... we used to sing, doubled up with giggles while Margaret tried to look unamused. Around him was a wasteland, littered with the debris of what had once been stores, cinemas and restaurants along the Moor.

At one end of the centre in no-longer existing Fitzalan Square there had been a pub, the Marples they called it. Their customers had taken shelter in the cellars in the first *blitz* of December 1940 that had done all the damage. That was coming up to my second Christmas in Cork, where I didn't hear so much as a car backfiring.

A seven-story building must be safe, people thought. A direct hit had collapsed it on top of them and the bottles of spirits burst and caught fire. Dad heard the screaming, he said. They dropped fifty tons of quicklime onto the site after this.

Mum and Dad had been in the city centre on that Thursday night. A message flashed up on the cinema screen that bombers were approaching. As before, they thought they were on their way to Manchester. It was a frosty night and the Dorniers followed the gleaming tram lines from Meadowhead right into the centre of town. When the Gaumont started shaking from the explosions and blasting, they ran across the road to an air raid shelter under the Grand Hotel. This place had five floors and was also considered safe.

On the steps of the City Hall nearby was a static water tank, a swimming pool-sized water store in case the mains were ruptured by the bombs. There were a lot of these around the city. They were about six feet deep and kids drowned in them. This particular tank was hit by a bomb that night and the water had flooded the cellars of the Grand Hotel up to their knees, Dad said.

Then the police came in and shouted for a doctor. Dad put his hand up but said he had no bandages or stuff, so a sergeant told him they would go down to Boots. They went down Fargate, past a tram upside down and burning and the sergeant slung a paving stone through Boots' window. He then shone his flashlight so Dad could see to pile stuff from the dispensary into a cardboard box. Then they went back to the Grand. Dad said it was so bright from the fires you could see the German bombers, like little flies, cruising over the city.

A few of the casualties died on him and the police lifted them out into Barkers Pool and laid them on the war memorial plinth. Most injuries were just cuts and broken bones and with help from Mum and others he got them sorted.

When we finally got home from Liverpool it was to a new house in Greenhill in a much nicer part of

Sheffield. During the *blitz* our old house had fifty bombs dropped within half a mile of it but didn't have so much as a smashed window. The only real drama, Mum said, was the back yard piled high with Sheffield plate on the morning after the first air raid. Teapots, cigarette cases, cups and plates blasted there from a bomb hitting a nearby factory, lay shining like pirates' treasure. The nursemaid and Paddy and baby David had huddled in the cellar and when Mum got back at five in the morning from her and Dad being caught in the centre of Sheffield, they were all asleep. So she left them there and they didn't wake up until dinner time.

Dad had left the old practice as well and set up on his own, using the lounge as a consulting room. The dining room was the waiting room and the pantry was the dispensary. All of us crowded into the little kitchen when surgery started.

Michael had to go to hospital with diphtheria. This was serious, for him and for Dad's practice. It was very infectious and the Health people said his patients could not visit the house until it had been fumigated. We had to move out and went to stay at Uncle Ged's surgery in a big old house in Devonshire Street in the centre of town. It was on the edge of the bombed area which was vast and stretched as far as you could see in all directions.

On the Sunday we were there it was hot. Suddenly there was a commotion. Four fire engines came along and the firemen started squirting water on the rubble. We were not allowed out but from our bedroom window saw a river of brown moving across the road. Dad said that all the rats living in the bombed area had eaten everything in the demolished shops and decided to migrate. They picked West Street as their new home.

The Health people calculated two million rats were on the move. The only thing the firemen could do was stop those rats that wanted to go off on their own. They were sent back into the main stream of animals with blasts of water. Dad said they wanted them all together so the rat-catchers knew where to work and which sewers to poison and so on.

On my way from Cork to Dublin, Policewoman Aileen bought me a comic for the boat. One of the picture stories was of a man locked in a cellar screaming as rats came in and ate him down to the bone. Aileen said it was fantasy and I wasn't to worry. As a *Garda* I knew she was telling the truth but after what I saw at Devonshire Street I wasn't so sure and was glad when we were back in our new home.

For weeks I lay in bed worrying about things. If it wasn't German bombers it was rats running in and eating me up. Mum said I was a worrier and I said after what I'd seen I had good cause to worry. I wanted to go back to Auntie Mary's where there were no German bombers. She told me to go out and play but that was kids' stuff and not what I wanted to do. To keep me quiet, or maybe because she was worried, she said she knew someone who had a bike to sell and gave me three pounds to go and get it.

I stopped worrying when I got the bike because

I was free to go where I wanted then. I knew I couldn't go back to Cork but still day-dreamed about putting some old inner tubes around it and floating across.

Ireland quickly become a memory. A memory of soft rain and green fields and fresh breezes from the sea pouring into your lungs, giving you a lift in spite of your troubles and making you glad to be alive. It wasn't all wonderful but when you thought back on it you made it that way.

The shawlies you scorned became romantic. The drunkards weaving their way home humming silly ditties made you smile. The crowds pouring out of Mass every morning of the week made you feel guilty you hadn't been one of them. The men to whom the inside of a church was a woman's place and the outside where they laughed and smoked, the man's world. And how the women would kneel at the Sanctus bell and drag themselves back on their feet after the third bell and carry on where they left off.

Now bombed-out Sheffield was the reality, a grey, grimy and gritty reality. Shabby women who had no coupons for clothes. Utility furniture, queues, always queues and pitch dark streets after dusk. Big Ss and arrows pointed to air raid shelters. It was also back to tenpence-worth of sweets a month and dried egg like gobs of yellow plasticine. Sirens wailed regularly with a sound that could precipitate the moving of your bowels and begin the race to get yourself on the toilet before you let go.

Balloons were still tethered around the city, like gigantic teardrops waiting to fall. At night the searchlight operators would use them as targets and make them look like Christmas tree lights. I began to get a bit bored with how drab and dirty it all was and kept thinking about the green fields around Cork and trips out West and the fresh air off the Atlantic Ocean in your face.

There was an airfield about a mile away from our house and I started going up that way across the fields to see what was happening. Nothing much was. It seems it was too small for the RAF so it was being used as a sports field for the Sheffield Transport Department.

In one corner, however, in the Norton direction was what looked like a prison camp. Tall posts with barbed wire ran all around it. Mum said it wasn't a prison camp but a detention centre for naughty American airmen. There had been a series of air raids conducted by the American Air Force on Schweinfurt southern Germany where most of their ball-bearings was made. The Americans thought if they could destroy these factories the war would be over a lot sooner.

Even though hundreds of American and RAF aircraft and crews were lost, raids on the town continued. Some of the American crews decided they'd had enough and nipped over the border to neutral Switzerland to get away from the *flak* and the fighters. Eventually there were hundreds of American aircraft parked up on Swiss airfields and their crews went into comfortable internment.

Sometimes on the way to raids, some of the crews wanted to go straight to Switzerland and some didn't. There would be fights which were resolved by the captain taking his pistol out. When they landed back in Britain the erring airmen were sent to the Norton Detention Centre to help them get their courage back. This was hush-hush. The Americans didn't want such things known about.

The detainees had it quite easy. At least, that was how it looked from the outside. They lazed around during the day and were allowed out in the evenings but no further than a mile away from the camp. To ensure this was observed Army Air Force 'snowdrops' patrolled. They were military police with white luminous helmets and batons like the police have in American films and if there was any fighting when the airmen came out of the local pubs, heads were bashed in. Generally, the detainees were well-behaved and people around liked them.

Their big problem was girls, or lack of them. As well as being confined, they lost pay. Either way, they couldn't stroll around Sheffield city centre with a girl on each arm like other Yanks. They just hung around at the camp gates.

I found them to be nice guys and friendly and went up there a lot to chat to them. They called me 'kid' and asked if I had any sisters and did I know any girls. Sometimes they would go to their PX and buy me chewing gum. That was great, since gum was difficult to get and I once exchanged a rabbit for just one stick from a boy near us.

With memories of Cork docks never far away I

soon felt temptation whispering. I had no big sisters and Jean didn't count and was still in Ireland anyway but I had friends who had. As my bike needed repairing I said I might be able to bring a girl or two up but it could be expensive. The half-crown I suggested for each date was met with great enthusiasm. It was so easy!

About a mile away there was a recreation field on which we used to meet up and kick a ball around. Sisters out of sheer boredom I think, would sit on the fence around the ground and watch. When the game was over I would stroll across and with my well- practiced Blarney, talk to them about the great table-tennis games I could fix up with the Americans at the camp.

Well, do bees like honey? There were few local men, as most were away in the forces. It was five miles and an uncertain tram ride to the dance hall and at the two cinemas there could be queues hundreds of yards long for each house. The last one was late, at eight-fifteen. There was one other gathering place, the local chip shop. This had no lights outside because of the blackout. The one inside went off and on automatically when the door was opened and closed.

On the first night, I took three girls up to the camp. That was a good number because they could cover for each other about being in a friend's house. Their mothers couldn't cross-check because most people didn't have 'phones and it was pretty safe for them. The airmen were waiting at the gates. They were under a promise to see the girls home again as best they could after their ping-pong. That was a cool seven shillings and sixpence and I was on the way to making a fortune.

As the evenings drew in, the girls were nervous of going out in the dark and I was appointed leader. A gaggle of them would gather round me and with my torch sweeping the lane, off we would go. I would stay at the camp until it was time to escort them back. I'd sit around or play darts with some of the airmen or watch the table tennis. Most of the girls would leave home in slacks but would change into little skirts for playing in and I liked looking at them leaping around the table. It took me back to Clare O'Reilly and her friends in the attic at Nicholas Well Lane.

Sometimes one or two of the girls would disappear for a while but this didn't bother me. None of them made a pass at me, though. I was like a kid brother and although they might give me a kiss when they got home it was in the way sisters do it.

After three months I had made about fifteen pounds. I kept it in a tin in my bedroom and when Mum found it one day when cleaning I explained it was present money from Cork. She looked at me suspiciously. When I came home with a brand-new Wigfalls Royal, a Wiggy's gas pipe we called them, she didn't say anything even though it had cost me seven pounds ten shillings.

Everything fell apart just before Easter. I was having my breakfast. Dad was in the lounge doing surgery and Mum was upstairs feeding my new sister. There was a knock on the back door and two policemen walked in.

"Neil Murphy?" The taller of the two grabbed me by the scruff of the neck, almost lifting me off the ground. Dad just happened to be coming through to his pantry dispensary. As a full-blooded Irishman he had a paranoia about policemen and let out a roar. In attempting to wrestle me out of the policeman's grip he slipped and fell onto the range.

Mum came in with Teeny in her arms and brought some order. Checking the last patient had gone she ushered us down the hall and into the dining room, sat us down and shut the door on Paddy and David who were leaning over the banister, their eyes popping out.

The policeman with silver-grey hair took a deep breath and turned to Mum and Dad. "Your son has been soliciting girls for the Americans at the Norton Camp."

A shiver ran down my spine and my stomach turned. I was in trouble again. I don't suppose he could have expressed it any other way

"We've had a complaint, a girl on Annersley Road. Her mother tells us she's pregnant, pregnant after going to the camp, taken there by your son." He pulled out a notebook. "Your son's been picking up girls for money."

Mum gasped. "Money ... that new bike ..."

Dad shook his head, removed his glasses and wiped his eyes.

"We sent him off to Ireland at the outbreak. He was six. Only six. It was a mistake but how do you know? With all the bombs it seemed the best thing to do."

This was followed by a long silence during which time Mum was white-faced and Dad flummoxed.

"What now?" Mum asked nervously.

Silver-grey shook his head. "We can't take him to court because of his age. Bringing him before the magistrate should be avoided, so it might be best if he admits to it all. Then he'll receive a talking to. He'll need to come to Woodseats Police Station. See the Inspector."

"Now?" Mum stood up.

'Tomorrow, Missers Murphy. And now if one of you can sit in, we'll take his statement."

Chapter Thirteen

I was to go to De La Salle College, my senior school, in the Autumn of 1943. Mum thought I should fill in at the local council school for the last part of the Summer Term and Summer holiday if possible. But once they found out I had a brother who was in Lodge Moor Hospital with diphtheria, they decided they didn't have a place for me.

Well that's how Mum explained it. But, it wasn't quite like that. What really happened was that during assembly at my first day at the council school the headmaster called me onto the stage and in front of the whole school said I had come from a filthy home. Because of that my brother was dying of diphtheria which was a terrible illness.

Ever since kissing the Blarney Stone I had lost my shyness and when he came up with this, I shouted that he was a liar and that Michael had diphtheria because Dad was a doctor and people with germs came to see him and some of the germs had been passed on.

The headmaster got angry and said I was insolent and taking out his strap he grabbed my hand and gave it a real wallop. It hurt and I started crying and because I was crying in front of everyone I got angry and shoved him and he fell off the stage and bumped his head. Then everyone cheered and I ran away. Next day, Mum got a letter saying I was expelled.

Mum, realizing now she had a goose among her swans certainly didn't want me hanging around until the Autumn with the likelihood of me getting into further trouble. I knew my parents blamed themselves for my conduct. Mum kept saying they shouldn't have sent us away. I understood that but not the business about my asthma and the psychosomatic stuff.

Dad, who was a caring doctor but silly at times, decided the best way to cure my asthma was by shouting "stop ..." at the end of the bed if I started wheezing and choking. That didn't work and usually meant a ride in an ambulance to the Children's Hospital with my chest heaving and black spots floating in front of my eyes. Fortunately they had a new drug there so I didn't need an iron lung. In a matter of hours I would recover and be back home. In the end he gave up and, in response to Mum's urging, sent me off to Spout.

In those days rich people had a farm for tax pusposes, whatever that meant. As Dad had a number of these so-called farmers on his list they decided to trawl through them. They were soon in luck. A 'little mester', what Sheffielders called steel and cutlery manufacturers who operated from slummy Victorian premises and made a lot of money out of the war, would be delighted to give Doctor Murphy's son work on his farm during the summer. And as he was going there the next weekend with his family I could go with them.

Mr. Rumble was a short, round man. He sported a moustache, wore a tweed suit and to the fat, unlit cigar in his mouth looked every inch a bookie. But he wasn't a bookie, he was a steel-maker. And for anyone who associates steel-making with blast furnaces and rolling ingots, if they visited his place glorified by a sign the length of the building proclaiming Rumbles Steelworks, they would be very disappointed. The establishment was located in a Victorian terrace of back-to-back houses. Two of these had been made into one by knocking out the inside walls. There was no upstairs floor and the roof sagged in parts and bulged in others.

The cellar which was essential. A hole had been cut in the ground floor and a pit created from firebricks. The hole at the base of the pit in the cellar had fire bars across it to stop the burning material falling through. And that was it.

The making of steel, which I had witnessed a few days earlier on an introductory visit, consisted of placing scrap iron in a fireclay pot about the size of a milk span in this pit, piling coke around it and lighting it with wood, paraffin oil and a burning newspaper. The high technology part was opening the cellar door into the garden. The draught roared up through the furnace until the steel was melting.

More scrap iron was dropped in followed by some mysterious powders in a paper bag. Then everyone went off to the pub. On returning, the pot would be white hot, so hot you couldn't look at it without blue glasses. The 'melter' who was covered in sacking which he soaked in a water trough, pulled the thing from out of the furnace with chain, pulley and tongs and poured its contents into an iron mould. Then they all went home after a heavy day's work.

What surprised me was that Mr. Rumble made enough money to send his kids to private schools, to have a big house in the best part of Sheffield and to drive a Rolls-Bentley.   It was a matter of licenses, he explained. Companies licensed their discoveries to others to use, for a price. Even Vickers used a Krupp-designed shell fuse during the Great War and were obliged in 1926 to make a back-payment of royalties owed.

There was an even more bizarre situation with English Steel up the road. They were using a German drop-hammer to make Spitfire crankshafts. The hammer was so important it had an armed guard around it day and night against possible German sabotage.

Well, it seems Rumbles Steelworks had, before the war, taken out a license with another German company to use their formula for a super-steel very useful in aircraft engines. Rumbles Steelworks didn't have to produce much of it, Mr. Rumble said proudly. Just one of the sixty-pound ingots was enough to keep the aircraft industry going for two days. I decided this was the line I wanted to be in.

On the Saturday morning after my introduction to Sheffield steel-making I stood on our drive waiting to be picked up. Mum had packed my bag and my inhaler and put five shillings in my pocket. Then she gave me a most embarrassing kiss as Rumble's Rolls-Bentley slid up to the gate.

Mr. Rumble jumped out and opened the back door. The car was absolutely stuffed and I could hardly get in. Because rationing demanded that no matter how rich you were, you took your own food with you, half the back seat was covered in groceries. There were boxes, bags and bottles, even toilet rolls. To justify his journey if he was stopped by the police, the boot was filled with seed potatoes for the farm.

Then there was their daughter, Angela, languishing across beige chamois leather. Long legs, very long legs and long blonde hair. Very long blonde hair. And in between, a brown tweed suit and a thin, pale face that stared at me through heavy glasses giving me the impression she could smile if she could be bothered.

As her father shut the door she turned her back on me and opened a magazine. We were off to the Lake District. It was over a hundred miles away and the thought of being stuck with Angela's back all that way wasn't very appealing. But at least she smelled nice. With a rich father you can, I suppose, obtain the best quality Black Market perfumes.

As we set off, Mrs. Rumble, a fat jolly lady commanded me to shake her podgy hand. It was a hot and sweaty hand and there were so many rings on her fingers I couldn't imagine it peeling potatoes.

"I'm Margery Rumble, Neil. You can call me Missers Rumble. And beside you is Angela." She raised her voice. "Angela, say hello to Neil!"

The girl twisted her head and looked at me for ages, not, I felt because she wanted to but because she wanted me to feel silly. She mumbled hello and returned to her magazine.

Comparing Mr. Rumble's car to Dad's Morris would I felt, be a sin. In fact it would have been an insult to Mr. Rumble to try. No matter how bad the roads were over the moors with tanks having churned up the tarmac, the car took it in its stride. We swished smoothly up and down the mountain roads and you could hardly hear the engine.

It was as we were motoring through Carlisle and I was dozing from being up early, that I became aware of Angela's thigh against mine. I was wearing shorts because Mum thought the Boy Scout image suited. At first I thought it was Angela getting comfortable. But then it started again, a slow rubbing. To be sure, I made a gap between us. The gap was slowly closed. I held my breath but stopped that as I didn't want to bring on an asthma attack.

Then I became aware of something else happening. Clare O'Reilly had joked about what happens to boys when there was a bit of cheekiness. It seems Angela Rumble knew about it as well as I could see her looking sideways at the disturbance created by her thigh rubbing.

When her hand moved over and patted my disturbance I gasped. She carried on reading her Girls' Weekly as if she had no other interest. Then another patting and a gentle stroking as if I had creases that needed smoothing. My breathing deepened. I thought I should ask her to stop but it was too late. I let out a groan and wriggled like a hooked maggot.

"What?" Mrs. Rumble looked around. "Are you alright, Neil?"

The hand disappeared. "I, er, was just coughing."

Angela looked at me slyly and slipped her handkerchief to me, the one she had been giving little coughs into. She put her lips to my ear and whispered, "dirty little boy ..."

"What is that smell?" Mrs. Rumble sniffed deeply. "You did shower this morning, Percy?"

"I, er ..."

Angela jumped in. "It's pickle, Mummy. The jar's leaking. Smells awful doesn't it?" Digging in her bag she pulled out a small scent spray and injected a sweet-smelling cloud into the car.

"Now it smells like a bloody brothel ..."

"Percy! Remember Doctor Murphy's son is with us!"

As Mrs. Rumble looked to the front again I felt something cold and sticky down my leg. Oh God! There was a wet stain from my fly buttons down. Angela grinned slyly from the safety of Girls' Weekly.

"Keep the hanky," she whispered again. "Bring it to my bedroom tonight. I'm going to smack your bottom, you dirty little boy ..."

I cleaned myself up as best I could, stuffed the hanky in pocket and sat grinning for the next half-hour.

It was at a sign to Crossthwaite, just five minutes

from our destination when we saw a police car blocking the road and a policeman with his hand raised.

"Oh, God! Just what we didn't want."

Mr. Rumble pulled up and got out but was back moments later dabbing his face and neck with a hanky. He grinned briefly at his wife. It was nothing to do with petrol or seed potatoes, or piles of food in the back. An aircraft had crashed up ahead. The road was narrow and they were keeping it clear for the emergency services. The Westmoreland constable had apologised for delaying us and hoped we were not inconvenienced. I wondered if he would have been so polite if we'd been in the Morris.

As it was so hot we all got out. I went and lay on the grass on my front. We were in a valley with fells on either side of us. Cloud across the summits was descending the silver becks in ghostly grey fingers, teasing away their shine and leaving thin veils drifting over the dark green forests. The bleating of sheep mixed with the bubbling of the stream by the road. There was the murmuring of machinery some way away. I could smell freshly-cut grass and paraffin smoke from the tractor cutting it.

Suddenly Mr. Rumble called out, "there's Spout!" He was sitting on the running board but stood up pointing at a cluster of buildings on a hillside in the distance. "And there ... my God ... is the vicarage ..."

Mrs. Rumble let out a little scream.

On the roof of the dark Victorian building below the farm, resting as if it had been placed there by a crane was a silver P51 Mustang fighter with its wings hanging over the gutters. There was no smoke. No fire. It must have been flying very slowly when it dropped. Fetching binoculars from the glove box Mr. Rumble focussed on the scene.

"Amazing! Quite amazing. It's smashed the roof but not gone deep inside. The roof trusses are supporting it."

"Oh, poor Reverend Vavasor. Is he alright?"

"I can't see the family but I shouldn't think they've come to any harm."

"And the pilot?"

"Doesn't look good." Half a dozen firemen were struggling with the cockpit hatch. "They're lifting him out but it doesn't look as if he's made it."

Mr. and Mrs. Thompson were waiting for us when we arrived. Mr. Rumble's manager was a tall man with a thin, tired face. He was wearing manure-spattered trousers stuffed into Wellingtons and a straw and hayseed-flecked jacket held together with binder twine. Mrs. Thompson was a mirror image of Mrs. Rumble, dumpy and cheerful. She was very welcoming but I felt her husband was not so happy to see us.

The hillside on which the farm stood was so steep you got the impression it was about to fall on you. Up from the farm was short grass, long bracken, broken rocks and nibbling sheep. It was the lower half that made the money. Large fields, some grassed and some ploughed, went all the way down and across the road. There were more fells beyond and the jagged blue peaks of the western Lake District. In all, the 'estate' ran to a hundred acres with half of it good for nothing but sheep.

Mr. Rumble undid his jacket, thrust his thumbs behind his braces and nudged me towards Mr. Thompson. "This is Neil, Thompson. Work him hard while he's with us. A bit prone to mischief when he's bored."

He followed this immediately with a comment about the posts still being in the fields. At the outbreak of war all fields over an acre had posts cemented in them to deter enemy gliders from landing, as had happened in the German occupation of Belgium and Holland. But they were a nuisance and had caused accidents with tractors. Since the German invasion of Russia, the threat had receded and the War Ag had ordered their removal.

Thompson struggled with a scowl. "I am busy, Sir, very busy. Since the Land Girls have gone I'm almost on my own."

"What about the prisoners?"

"Eyties, Sir. Bloody Italians. They're little use."

Rumble's piggy eyes narrowed but he didn't launch into a confrontation with his manager with his family present. "Well, you've got Neil now. He'll take some of the weight off your shoulders."

"Yes, Sir." Thompson's look showed clearly he didn't think so.

"Into the house now." Mrs. Thompson began bustling. "Tea's set in your room, Missers Rumble. And perhaps you could show this young man where he'll be in the barn, Arthur?"

The two women went inside and the men unloaded the car. I was eyeing up the dilapidated barn when Angela came quietly up beside me, Girls' Weekly still in hand and whispered "my room's at the end of the landing in the house. Turn left at the top of the stairs. The green painted door ... "

I was learning what a wicked look was but didn't know how thrilling it could be when directed at you.

Mr. Thompson pointed up the wooden steps inside the barn. "Go on up. It's comfortable, I promise ye. The Land Girls liked it. We used to have two but we couldn't keep them ... " he nodded back towards the yard "... decided they were too expensive. So off they went to Barrow shipyard."

"But I like Angela!" I said grinning.

He gave me a long look. "Best watch out, Neil. She can be a bit fresh, lead you on. It goes with her TB, you know."

"TB?"

"Didn't you notice her coughing, spitting blood?"

"Blood?"

He nodded. "Best watch yourself."

He turned at the barn door. "And don't forget you're surrounded by hay and straw. There's no electric, so its candles. Start a fire and we'll be having you for dinner, with an apple in your mouth!"

There were four beds with straw palliasses in the lime-washed loft area. There were massive dusty beams, chinks of light coming through the roof and gaps between the floorboards. There were a few bits and pieces of girls' stuff on an old dressing table. A roof light without a blind directly above meant I would be woken at first light.

Picking a bed I threw myself on it and stared at the sky. I thought about the Mustang pilot and how his head had flopped, like Finnegan's. I watched the clouds drifting by and listened to the shuffling and snorting of the cows in the byre below. I pulled out Angela's handkerchief and opened it. Lipstick stains and, yes, there between the crimson outlined lip shapes were dark, almost black spots. I wasn't very happy about that and dropped it under the bed. Then I fell asleep.

It was getting dark when I woke because of a shout from below. Supper was ready. I'd better hurry or I would miss it.

The farmhouse was split in two. The Thompsons' half was small, comfortable and clean. The flagged floor was covered in rag rugs, a large clock ticked on the wall and a cast iron range was stuffed with logs glowing red through its bars. Wood smoke filled the air. Mrs. Thompson smiled welcomingly and pointed to what would be my place at the table. I felt seriously hungry and the pork pie and hard-boiled eggs looked inviting. Tea was poured into brown mugs and never tasted so good.

Talk was of the crashed plane. Mr. Thompson said he had watched it come down and but for two feet, would have made it into the field. A wing tip had clipped one of the chimneys and it had spun round. The fuel tanks held so house, vicar and family had survived. Not that the man would have been missed, he snorted. Shell-shocked from the Liverpool bombing he now stuttered in front of a congregation.

The fire officer reckoned the pilot was caught by thick cloud suddenly descending and had come low along the valley. Seeing he was trapped and possibly lost, he probably decided on an emergency landing. As his flaps and undercarriage were down his speed was low and he just flopped.

After tea we stood in the yard looking towards the vicarage. The firemen had rigged up floodlights and were emptying the fighter's fuel tanks. Mr. Thompson wasn't suited. He and a couple of locals had planned to do the job themselves as soon as it was dark. Then we went in and listened to the news that was all about the Russians smashing the German army.

Mrs. Thompson gave me a torch to see my way back to the barn. I had a good wash in the yard trough and went into the loft and changed. The water and evening air was bracing and I was game for anything. Coming back down to the farmyard I stood watching the lights in the house go out one by one until it was in darkness. I left it a little while longer then crept back across the yard, opened the front door and listened. As there was only some muted snoring I crept upstairs. I felt a bit giddy.

The stairs were solid and there was no creaking. At the top I fumbled along the walls to the left as Angela said and reached the end where a little window admitted a glow from a crescent moon peaking over the dark outline of the hills.

A brief flash of my torch confirmed the green door and with gentle pressure on the latch it swung open. I heard some deep breathing and as I crept across the floor, there was a creaking of bedsprings. Fumbling across the bed I found her feet and squeezed gently.

"I've come to have my botty smacked ..." I whispered.

There was a stirring. The blankets heaved, a scraped match burst into flame and a candle was lit.

"I'm here," I whispered eagerly.

"And I'm here?" Mrs. Rumble, her head covered in a cap stared curiously at me. "Bottle smashed? Just sweep it up then, don't bother me." Out went the candle, up went the blankets and the gentle snoring resumed.

When I got up, Angela was putting her bag into the car. She was going to a school friend's at Kendal and wouldn't be back until after the weekend. Mrs. Rumble was sitting on an old bench outside the kitchen door with a cup of tea admiring the view. "Not much for Angela here, is there? It's a rest for Percy and me too. The poor man works so hard."

She sipped her tea. "That bottle. Did you manage to clear it up?"

"I came in for my tooth brush and bumped into the dresser. Did you hear the crash?" I had worked out my response to the inevitable questions and it went off without a hitch.

"I sleep like a log. Country air. What was it?"

"Slippery stuff. Smelt like perfume."

"Angela's shampoo probably. Not to worry, she can pick up some more in Kendal."

As we were talking, an army lorry in green camouflage roared up to the gate and a soldier with a rifle and bayonet dropped from the cab and pulled at the canvas flap at the rear. A soldier in drabs jumped out. Mrs. Rumble put her tea down and got to her feet.

"Luciano!"

"*Ah, Signora!*" As the soldier stumbled towards her he pulled some sandwiches from a brown paper parcel and started breaking bits off for the hens that had appeared magically. "Spam. It's Spam again. If I knew I would be fed Spam I would never have surrendered!"

He put the sandwiches back in his pocket, put his hands on Mrs. Rumble's shoulders and kissed both her cheeks. "*Bella Signora. Bella* Missers Rumble. I asked to come back to work here again!"

You could guess Luciano was Italian. He looked like all Italians I had ever seen and was just as cheerful. Mr. Thompson had come out of the barn with the arrival of the lorry and stood watching, chewing on a stalk of corn that moved across his face from left to right and back again.

"And this," Mrs. Rumble gestured towards me, "is Neil. He's going to help with the heavy work."

"Hello, helping boy," Luciano said with a big smile, putting his hand out. The morning sun was clearing the mist rapidly and making Luciano's black, shiny curls and his eyes flash.

"You a strong boy?"

I had believed since the beginning of the war that Italians, because they were with the Germans, were

217

enemies. He didn't look like one to me. He just seemed to be a nice guy. Mrs. Rumble thought so too.

"Would you like a cup of tea, Luciano?"

"No, no, kind lady. I work now. Mister Thompson is waiting, I see." He turned to me. "And you come too, helping boy!"

As we entered the barn, Mr. Thompson didn't bother with any greeting. He thrust hayforks into our hands. "Bottom field," he said brusquely. "Cock the hay. We need to get it in before the rain starts."

"Okay, Mister Thompson, Sir. We start immediately!"

We walked into the yard where Angela was waiting by the car for her Dad. She greeted Luciano with a warm smile and cheek kisses also. She turned to me, looked at my pitchfork and said "my, that's a big weapon you have there!"

I turned away, a little shocked.

"Sulking, are we!"

"You sent me to your mother's room."

Her eyebrows lifted in mock astonishment. "Tell me about the 'smashed bottle'?" she giggled. Coming close she whispered in my ear. "You're just a dirty little boy, aren't you?"

I felt colour flooding into my cheeks. "And you're a right bitch," I said under my breath.

"*Oo la la!*" She flicked her fingers theatrically. "Did you hear what he called me, Luciano?"

Luciano, watching our altercation with great interest held up his hands. "'Tis not true, pretty *signorina*. But I think you have not been kind to him?"

"I could be kind to you, Luciano. Very kind!"

She walked off, wiggling her hips and slid into the front seat of the car. As the car left the farmyard in a cloud of dust, Luciano sighed deeply. "If only I wasn't a prisoner. But that is how things are. Damn Mussolini to Hell!"

We worked hard that morning and by the time we were called up to the house for lunch the field was lined with pimply haycocks waiting for the dray. I was sodden with sweat but Luciano took it in his stride. He had been at the camp for a year and was used to being a farmer's boy. At times he would also fill his lungs and share a verse with the birds, the nearby cows or the trees. And frequently the wind-driven branches would applaud. I think Mr. Thompson had got it wrong about Eyties being little use.

In odd moments he would advise me on how I should handle girls like Angela and ladies in general. Like all Italians, he said, he was very interested in ladies. He had a wife and two kids in Florence he told me but that was a long way away and likely to remain so for a while.

He was an aircraft fitter with the *Regio Aeronatica*, their equivalent to the RAF. He had been serving in the North African desert and when it was clear our Eighth Army would over-run them, they came out of their forts swathed in white sheets. They saw no shame in it. He and his comrades thought war was a stupid way of carrying on anyway when there was wine, pasta and lovely women to enjoy in the countryside.

All the Italians, he told me, liked England. They were not like the *Tedesci*, as he called the Germans, who were in another camp, half a mile away. He thought they were a sad bunch. He found it incredible they spent most of their spare time drilling with mock rifles made from poles.

As we sat in the kitchen over our stew and doorstep chunks of bread he never stopped talking and it was clear Mrs. Thompson couldn't have enough of his charm. Mr. Thompson was not so taken and as soon as we had cleared our plates he would edge us back towards the door. Lunchtimes became very short.

Over the next weeks we got all the hay into stacks with no problems from the weather. Then we had the corn to cut. Luciano drove the tractor and I picked up the sheaves that tumbled from the reaper and binder. I leaned the sheaves of corn against each other, six at a time making stooks for the dray cart which would take them to the barn for threshing. The work was tiring but helped by good food I was getting stronger. Despite the dust I never once used my inhaler and felt my asthma was a thing of the past.

The harvest was in by the middle of that September, 1943. While we waited for the threshing engine we turned our attention to the turnips. They were to be lifted before the frosts came but before that happened they had to be weeded and singled.

The hoeing was dreary and Luciano's boredom with it showed. Then, with a chill in the air and leaves turning golden and the sky a sharper blue, he became noticeably sullen.

Sitting down for our afternoon break at the edge of the field he said, "I think I escape. Go home. I have decided." He looked at me challengingly. "You come too?"

"To Italy?"

"Of course, Italy!" Opening his jacket he pulled out a map. "I can get a British uniform. Go down south. Get on a boat. It will be easy. I will take my friends. You are my friend. Okay?"

"How will you get out of the camp?" I had seen the towers and searchlights. There were guns. There could be shooting.

"Ah," he flicked his hand, "we will get out."

"But how?"

He stood up looked around the fields carefully and said "come, I show you."

Keeping to the hedge we hurried down the road to the vicarage with its forlorn-looking Mustang still fixed to its perch. The disagreement over who was to shift it continued. It was an American 'plane the RAF insisted and they could do the job. The Americans said it was in RAF territory. The unfortunate Reverend Vavasor was still languishing with his family in a local hotel.

Nipping into the garden, Luciano scrambled up the ladder the fire brigade had left. I crept up after him and crawled along the wing. They were designed to support a five-ton aircraft so there should be no problem with us. As we got closer to the fuselage the structure gave a heart-sinking lurch. Chunks of roof and brickwork tumbled to the garden, then it settled. Luciano gave me a thumbs-up and indicated I should keep my head down.

Some tools had been left behind so, in a flash I had one of its wing-tip navigation lights in my pocket. There would be some swap possibilities at my new school. I also removed the altimeter from the cockpit, oblivious to the dried blood spattered over it.

While I was pilfering, Luciano had opened the flap on the port wing and in a matter of minutes one of the half-inch Browning machine guns, together with a belt of ammunition, was being hauled across the fuselage and down the ladder. Ten minutes later we were back in the turnip field.

It was the custom for farmers to give their prisoners some of their produce, so when the lorry came to collect Luciano that evening, the guard took no notice of the large sack with turnip tops sticking out of it. In fact, he even helped Luciano swing the sack over the tailboard. He waved a cheery goodbye. I had told him I couldn't go to Italy but wished him luck on his venture. That was the last time I saw him.

Angela, I saw twice more at Spout. Her TB was hopeless, Dad said and she died in the Autumn in Crimicar Lane Sanatorium. She stayed in my mind for a long time. I never got the chance to kiss her, or try to kiss her and had hoped this would happen. I learned a lesson from her I would never forget.

Chapter Fourteen

I returned home from my Summer in Spout in a police car. The Westmorland Constabulary had ordered me out of their county and taken me as far as their border with Yorkshire where I was met by and transferred to, a Sheffield City Police car. Mum had been crying and I was greeted by her tear-stained face. Both she and Dad were beside themselves. They had sent me away to Westmorland in the hope hard work and fresh air would keep me out of trouble. It hadn't worked out like that.

The crisis had come the morning after Luciano Aguzzoli had left Spout with the machine gun in his sack of turnips. I had been mucking out after milking and was just sitting down to breakfast when a police car, followed by an army staff car rolled into the farm yard.

"Trouble, here," Mr. Thompson frowned, looking at me. For five minutes or so he stood talking to the arrivals then, coming back in he jerked his thumb at me. "Into the parlour."

"Oh, my, what have you been up to?" Mrs. Thompson wrung her hands.

I shrugged. "Nothing I know of." I felt my eyes watering. I always seemed to get the blame for whatever happened. I couldn't think what it was this time. Then I found out.

Luciano's notion of an escape attempt was forgotten as soon as he was back in camp. The prisoners had, it seems, some home-made wine brewed from parsnips and a group of them decided to make a party of it that night and have a bit of fun. By late evening it was thought the Browning was just the thing. They lashed it onto a wheelbarrow with a battery stolen from the CO's car and trundled it around, to the delight of the internees.

They weren't sure if it would fire until Luciano, helpless with wine, decided to try. The target, the car from which they had stolen the battery, stood unattended in front of the guardroom. Giggling inanely he touched the wires. With an ear-splitting rat-a-tat-tat, the car was reduced to a heap of flaming scrap by the rounds in the belt.

The guards had panicked. Surmising an attack on the camp, 'phone lines were immediately red hot between other military bases in the county, sirens sounded, lorries and troops were lined up and a telex was despatched to the War Office. Within half an hour soldiers with fixed bayonets were advancing on the silent, darkened camp. It was like this because the internees had lost interest and the party-goers gone to bed. Everyone that is, apart from Prisoner Aguzzoli slumped over the mounted machine gun, snoring loudly.

My name had emerged as a mumbled "my little English friend'. Of course, it could only be me.

Mum and Dad were good about it, considering. They were intelligent people. The war was everyone's biggest concern and once it was over, things would, they believed, return to normal. That included me.

Dad was a good Dad but a bit soft. Never, during the twenty years I was at home, did he hit me. The worse treatment I received was being called a "useless shitarse" after I had come down early one Sunday morning to see a fox dragging off the big lump of beef Mum had left on the kitchen table. I stood there gaping. My soubriquet was delivered as, in response to my yells, he had rushed out into the garden in his pyjamas, shotgun in hand and executed not the offending fox but one of its cubs, leaving the vixen to carry away her ill-gotten gains to share with the rest of her brood in their den in the field.

The next night, in response to the killing of one of her offspring, she returned and out of pure spite, we think, broke into our hen house and killed twenty hens. The remaining six had fluttered up to the safety of the cherry tree but had died of shock from watching the slaughter beneath.

So, what were my parents to do now? After mulling over the problem with the help of some gin and tonic they decided Uncle Bill, now CO of Lindholme Bomber Station twenty miles away was the one to restore law and order.

It was a sensible decision from my point of view. Parents are not the right people for sorting out their delinquent children. Uncles are better and Uncle Bill was one of the best sorting-out uncles you could have. I liked him. I trusted him. He had flown across to Ireland to see me when it was thought I was dying. He was the kind of uncle every boy dreams of having.

He had been coming over for tea two or three times a month since being at Lindholme and always found time to have a chat with me in the garden. He often talked about Canada and his work as an engineer before the war. He never talked to me in the way most grown-ups talk to boys. It was as if we were in the same club.

On one of his visits he said he would very soon be leading his squadron over the house on a mission over Germany. That puzzled me because the North Sea and Dutch coast beyond, was east of Lindholme. We were west. They needed height before crossing the Dutch coast, he explained but couldn't climb quickly when heavily loaded. They got the height by setting off in the opposite direction in a long upward corkscrew. He said I would see. And I did.

Two days later, at about seven o'clock in the evening when we were having supper, we heard a continuous rumbling sound growing louder. Out of the house we went to see a long line of Lancasters crawling, it seemed and so low the house shook and windows rattled. Then the circling began. They moved so slowly you expected them to fall out of the sky. Round they went, higher and higher until we could hardly see them. Then the noise faded and the sky was empty.

We all stood on the drive watching after they had

gone, as though we expected them back a few minutes later. They were away, of course and we finished supper. We had seen bombers off before but knowing Uncle Bill was there made us all very quiet as some of those aircraft would not be coming back.

Mum fixed up a trip to Lindholme for the Sunday after the Spout episode. Dad had petrol coupons to drive around the area of his practice. If he went outside his area some accounting would be needed, with the possibility of his coupons being stopped and a hefty fine needing paying. To cover our trip to Lindholme he made up a big bottle of medicine and stuck a label on it, 'Wing Commander Russell. RAF Lindholme'. As a patient could easily be out of the practice area the medicine delivery should cover him if a Home Guard or keen Bobby was to stop him and ask questions.

We set off after early Mass. To reach Lindholme we had to drive through Sheffield, past Bawtry and along country lanes until we reached the black and yellow barrier. Uncle Bill was waiting to tell us a raid was on that night. It meant Lindholme would be isolated until the operation was over. If we went through the barrier we couldn't leave until the morning and because the 'phones were down, we wouldn't be able to ring Dad to let him know. Mum knew Dad would realize what had happened so she said fine. Uncle Bill then signalled to the man in the guardhouse, the barrier was raised and with Uncle Bill in the back seat we cruised over the graveled roads to the officers' mess.

Two spare bedrooms at the camp had been prepared for us by a batwoman, Aircraftswoman Gill but she preferred to be called Lily. The windows overlooked the airfield which seemed to be empty of 'planes. Apart from the soldiers manning the anti-aircraft cannon on the roof of each of the hangers there was no other sign of life. Uncle Bill said that as it was Sunday they would be having a lie-in but that everything would change after lunch when the bombers were being made ready for the night raid.

It was an hour to lunch so he took us to the parachute room. He explained that because of wear-and-tear and damp each parachute had to be unpacked, treated if necessary and re-packed on a regular basis. There were six long tables in the room with Waafs busy opening 'chutes, pulling them along the table full length and scrutinizing the white nylon, often with a magnifying glass. It was really important to avoid knots in the cords, so narrow belts filled with lead shot were used to hold down each length as it was inspected.

Uncle Bill said that although the maintenance of parachutes was very professional, few fliers, himself included, fancied the idea of using one and would rather take the risk of crash-landing than jump out, particularly if they were over Germany where fliers who parachuted down safely were sometimes lynched by the civilian population. He said that careful records were being kept of the names of those involved in these lynchings. This was possible because there were a lot of people in Germany who hated Hitler and who were passing on these details. After the war they would be charged with murder and, if it was proved, hanged.

I thought it all very horrible but he laughed and said if you were a careful pilot it wouldn't come to that. He was obviously in that category as he had flown nearly fifty missions without any of his aircraft having a nick in them.

Lunch in the mess was very informal. When they dined in the evening, which they were required to do at least once a week, they put on their Number Ones. Otherwise anything went. After the lunch gong sounded the men and a few women officers, strolled in looking very ragamuffinish, togged up in bits of flying uniform, battledress, open-neck shirts and so on.

The mess rapidly filled with blue tobacco smoke and subdued talk. I found it difficult to believe that most of them would be over Germany in a few hours being shot at from all sides. Looking around at their casual poses and laughing faces I don't think many of them did either. But maybe it was bluff. If it had been me in their place I think I would have felt too sick to eat.

Uncle Bill was at the top of the middle table, the CO's privileged place. Many of the diners sat at the bottoms of the adjoining tables so that, I suppose, their boss couldn't hear their chat. Others just sat willy-nilly. Mum, being a civvy, attracted some attention but nobody intruded. All were, of course, officers and gentlemen and ladies.

Although missing the soup but just in time for

the beef and Yorkshire pudding, one officer strolled in alone. He was unusually tall but as his shoulders sagged, he presented poorly, as though he was tired. He also seemed to be focussing on the floor, as if deep in thought. Although he had the broad stripe of a Flying Officer his gear looked very new. Going down the line of tables he seemed to be hesitant in finding a place. One or two signaled him to join them but he didn't appear to notice their gestures. Then, as he reached the end of the room he slipped out through the waiters' entrance and didn't return.

After the sweet, the room emptied. Because there was an op on, the bar was closed so there was no call for any of them to hang around. As we sat chatting I could see trolleys, ten or more in a line each cradling a bomb, being dragged out from blast-proof shelters by tractors and winding their way across the airfield to where the Lancasters were waiting to be fed.

"Time to be off." Uncle Bill clapped my shoulders. "You come with me and stick with me at all times. Your mother can wait in the mess." As we walked out of the door he pointed left. "Go and get yourself a parachute. Tell the sergeant I sent you."

"Parachute?"

"We're taking a little flight. A check flight. A new pilot joined us yesterday and I want to see if I can trust him with one of my crews. He's come well-recommended from OCT but you can't always trust their opinions. Sometimes they're just keen to get someone out of their hair!" He turned away as a Waaf came up with a signal which he signed.

"Which means we're definitely on."

While bombing missions were proposed by Command they were never definitely 'on' until a Mosquito had flown over the proposed target to check the weather. As the Mosquitos could fly at over 40,000 feet there was no risk from Bf 109s or *flak*. They had the run of the sky. Once they had signaled back, Command made the final decision. Uncle Bill had been given the go-ahead.

"Queenie Four. Over there." He pointed across the airfield. "Ten minutes."

As he went off with Mum I walked over to where the nose of a Lancaster emerged from its drape of camouflage netting. Standing waiting was that tall miserable-looking officer I had seen at lunch. Going up to him I introduced myself. When you got to know him, he wasn't miserable at all, just a bit shy. He was, he said, new at the station and didn't know anyone so rather than barge in on one of the lunch groups he had gone off and had a sandwich. He was older than me of course, but it didn't feel like it as we talked. He was a Sheffield lad. He and his Dad played golf at the same club as my Dad. He was a thirteen handicap and had a number of cups. And he knew my Uncle David whose factory he had worked at while waiting to get in the RAF.

Half a dozen mechanics were doing some checks as we chatted and one was wheeling up the 'trolley acc' which would start up the engines. He had just finished plugging in the cable when Uncle Bill arrived and waved us on board.

Climbing the little ladder I went forward to the

flight deck followed by my new friend whom Uncle Bill introduced as Flying Officer Cunningham. I was sent down into the nose, where the bomb-aimer normally lodges and Uncle Bill sat on the step at the side of the pilot. Headphones were plugged in, a switch closed and I could hear everything including the pilots breathing.

"How many hours have you done on Lancs, Cunningham?"

"Ten, Sir. And two leaflet drops."

"Ten? Is that enough for you to go on a mission, do you think?"

"I think so, Sir." Although he sounded confident, Uncle Bill didn't sound very enthusiastic.

"Think so? Well, let's see."

The four engines, beginning with the starboard outer, were fired up. The airframe was suddenly alive and throbbing, warm air began to flow through the cockpit. I took a deep breath, never having flown before. I had no idea how that great beast was going to get off the ground and stay up.

As we gathered speed down the runway I felt really exposed out front in a Perspex bubble with the concrete a blur not far below my feet. And then we tilted up slightly, the engines making an impressive noise and lifted off. It was an amazing sensation in my stomach, like being on a fairground ride. The trembling of the fuselage ceased, the engines dropped a note and we were flying as easily as a bird, fields and trees beneath us falling away. I had a queasy moment as we banked and there was suddenly not much between me and the moors far below but after this I settled back.

"Follow a course of two seven zero at five thousand feet." Uncle Bill's voice came over my headphones. "Watch out for ack-ack over Sheffield. Some of their observers could be stupid enough to have a pop at us, even though Jerry doesn't have any four-engined bombers."

"Sir."

From where I was lodged I could see past Uncle Bill into the cockpit. His eyes were alert but the rest of his face looked as relaxed as if he was sitting up in bed. His voice, calm but authoritative was just loud enough to be heard over the noise of the engines. Even though we were only going up to 5,000 feet oxygen masks were on because our mikes were embedded in them. Uncle Bill said nothing as we turned to starboard and headed west. Flying Officer Cunningham was in effect, on his own. I attempted some small talk but was politely told to switch my mike off.

There must have been close on a hundred barrage balloons over Sheffield. Even though the highest was five hundred feet below us they were still too close for comfort. As well as that, they gave you a real sensation of speed as you whipped past. Flying at height, Uncle Bill had explained, the ground seems to be drifting slowly by. It's only when you pass over a balloon, or something else static a few hundred feet below that you feel as though you are in land-speed record-breaking car.

The Derwent Valley dams, including Ladybower that was still filling up appeared on the horizon as

Sheffield slipped away behind us. These reservoirs had their moment of fame as a training facility for Guy Gibson and 617 Squadron for the attack on the Ruhr Dams the previous year.

As we cruised over the patchwork of green heather and brown bracken, occasionally racing through feathers of cumulus clouds Uncle Bill suddenly reached forward and shut off the starboard outer engine's throttle. The effect was dramatic. Deprived of a quarter of its power, People Queenie Four slewed right. The starboard wing dipped, the horizon began to turn and rise and I felt myself sliding as the aircraft began to plunge.

Then there was the bumping. As Uncle Bill explained later, that had occurred on crossing Derwent Edge running up from the dams. The westerly airflow, having nowhere else to go shoots up the cliff face like a fountain to pummel anything passing over it.

Without hesitation Flying Officer Cunningham pushed the stick forward to maintain speed, simultaneously feathering the prop of the idle engine to reduce its drag. He pushed open the other throttles and put left rudder on. We were back to straight and level within ten seconds.

"Well done." Uncle Bill made the comment quietly, reopening the fourth throttle. "You know what you're doing. "Now steer zero nine zero and let's get back for tea. You'll need it. You're flying tonight. Flight Lieutenant Keeley has gone down with a tummy bug. You'll be taking Alpha Romeo in his place. Your crew will be a bit on edge but I think you can put their fears at rest."

"Thank you, Sir. I will do my best."

I was mesmerized by the approach to the airfield again and a bit disturbed by the bump but it was a good landing I was told. Leaving the aircraft Uncle Bill and I wandered back to see Mum.

"Well!" he raised his eyebrows at me. "You've said nothing for a while!"

"Gave me a bit of a fright, the engine cutting out and the 'plane twisting."

"That's the important thing. How you behave when you've had a bit of a fright. That's when things can go badly wrong. You have to plan for frightening situations to stop them getting worse. Cunningham had done that. His response was spot on. He's a good man."

We walked on further, then he stopped and looked around at the ground crew busy with their work. "Planning, Neil, is what it's all about. Thinking ahead. Were you thinking ahead when you helped an Italian prisoner-of-war get his hands on a machine gun? Taking young girls to a military camp? No, you weren't. The list goes on. Not thinking ahead. You've caused a lot of trouble for a lot of people because ...?"

"I didn't think things through. Didn't think ahead."

"Okay, let's leave it at that. You've learned a lesson. Keep rehearsing it your mind. You've caused your mother a lot of grief. I'm relying on you not to let it happen again. Okay?"

"Okay." I grabbed his outstretched hand.

235

"Now, the AOC has given permission for you to attend the briefing! That's a special favour to me. It's at five o'clock. Be there on time." Turning away he went off to the admin block and I stood and watched him stride across the grass.

It was an important lesson for me. I was ashamed. I remembered Brother James's words in the hospital about staff losing their jobs because of the fire. My cousin Margaret from Douglas was one. My cousin Angela who brought me home had also worked there and was only able to do it because she was without a job. For years afterwards, whenever I thought of doing something wild, I would focus on the Grant's fire as I saw it from the Rock Steps. That would pull me up sharply.

The weather had been fine all day. The ground crew had stripped down to their shirts and were eyeing the off-duty Waafs sunning themselves on the grass outside the offices. But the Sheffield murk was slowly masking the sun's warmth and it was getting quite chilly as I found my way to the briefing room. SPs stationed outside were checking all entrants but having been given forward notice they waved me through.

The briefing room was the NAAFI, as it was the only place large enough to take the crowd of around a hundred and fifty people. A rostrum with a table on it had been placed at the serving end and the kitchens had been emptied of the girls in their nippy little uniforms. I felt a bit shy at being alone but as soon as F/O Cunningham came in I went and joined him. His eyes were bright and as he sucked at his cigarette I noticed his hand was trembling a little. He told me he had hiked a lot over the moors we had crossed and seeing it from 5,000 feet had given him a new perspective. Changed his point of view. I didn't really understand what he was talking about but I agreed. He said that next time he was on leave he would be walking over the same moors but with his fiancée. They were to be married at Easter and she would be staying in Doncaster to be nearer to him.

As we chatted, the hum of conversation swelled and the cigarette smoke thickened. Suddenly there was a shout and everyone rose to their feet. Uncle Bill and an important-looking officer with a broad, pale blue stripe on his cuff stepped onto the rostrum followed by a number of junior officers.

Uncle Bill held up his hand. "You all know our AOC and I'm going to hand you over to him first." Then he sat down.

"Good evening, gentlemen." The AOC leaned on the table and scanned the room to take in everyone present. "The Kamhuber Line!" A mild groan filled the room. This was the chain of anti-aircraft guns and radar-directed searchlights that stretched from Denmark to Paris to catch unwary pilots. "Cross it together. No straggling. If you're together their radar can't focus. It's useless. The war in the Atlantic was won using the convoy system. You use it too. I know you don't like close flying but while you're crossing that damned line, do it. And best of luck." At that he sat down.

Uncle Bill then stood up and pulled down the

roller blind behind him to reveal a map of Germany with different lines crossing it.

"Well, I'm sorry chaps but it's Berlin again." Then he raised his hand as more groans rippled across the room. "Okay. Leave it at that. No fuss."

Berlin was not popular, not only because it was the most dangerous but also because it was such a long trip. Ten hours was a long time for nerves to be on edge. Since the start of operations over Berlin, 500 British aircraft had been lost. This was because aircraft had a long period of vulnerability on the way in and because the city's air defences were awesome. Goering, attempting to defeat the bombers had built two massive *flak* towers from which guns stuck out like hedgehog spines.

Everyone dreaded their fire but, surprisingly, as it later turned out, an average 18,000 shells had been needed to down one aircraft. Their bark was worse than their bite! Nonetheless, the experience of flying over them was unnerving

Uncle Bill gave a run-down of the plan and invited the Navigating Officer, followed by the Met Officer and Signals Officer to fill in the details. You could feel the tension crackling. Banter had given way to silence and cigarettes were being lit, stubbed out half-smoked and replaced by another.

"Finally, chaps I'd like to welcome our newcomer." Uncle Bill gestured towards Flying Officer Cunningham. "He's joining Alpha Romeo as skipper tonight, as your captain's ill. He's an insert from Flying Command. Shot down all the Jerries so there was no more work for him there ..." A ripple of laughter went round the hall. "So you chaps get together. Best of luck."

With that, he was gone. Following his instructions I chased after him.

"Up into flying control. Through there," he said briskly, pointing to the door in the Control Tower. "Just sit quietly. I'll be with you shortly."

The control tower was glazed all round, giving a complete view of the airfield. I was directed to a vacant seat to watch the activity. Trolley accs, each with sufficient battery power to start all four engines of a Lanc trundled from the hangars to each of the dispersal islands where the aircraft squatted. Bombing-up was being finalized and through the binoculars given me I saw bomb doors closing. Crew were being shunted around in dirty grey busses and dropped off under the nose of their machines. I saw one of the pilots finishing off writing a letter, a small group was kicking a football around and other groups were chatting.

Looking at the plan pinned up in the Tower, I located Alpha Romeo and focused on my friend, still slack-shouldered but now in animated conversation with his new crew. As I watched, he looked at his wristwatch and nodded to his men to climb aboard. The door was pulled shut. A puff of black smoke was expelled from each engine in turn and the trolley ac disconnected. They were ready to move.

Going out onto the balcony of the Tower the control officer fired a green flare from his Very pistol and aircraft began taxiing towards the perimeter track to form a line to the runway. One after the other the hulking grey monsters began moving through the faint mist, like things pre-historic emerging from a swamp.

Uncle Bill came in and sat down without looking at me. "Are we ready?" He looked at his watch.

"Sir." The controller picked up his Aldis lamp.

Uncle Bill nodded. "Off with them, then. Let's get moving."

Returning to the balcony the officer aimed the little hand-held lamp at the first aircraft in line ready and waiting and signalled a green 'go'. Its engines opened up and it was almost immediately at a running pace. Just when you thought it wouldn't make it to the far end of the runway, the tail lifted and it floated off the ground. The controller aimed his Aldis lamp again. Another flash. Another Lanc started off down the runway. Then another.

Then Uncle Bill joined the controller on the balcony, as if he was expecting something to happen. The rhythm was suddenly broken. He came smartly back inside, picked up the mike and waited. It was very unusual for any R/T messages to be sent at this stage I had been told, as the German listening stations would have their ears cocked. As expected, a voice crackled through the loudspeakers in the Tower. "Charlie Delta returning. Mag malfunction."

"Stay where you are Charlie Delta. I will attend," Uncle Bill responded immediately. Pulling his jacket on he rushed down the tower steps with me on his heels, leapt into his car and told me to hold on tight.

A magneto is about the size of a large cocoa tin. Its job was to supply a nice fat spark to each of the plugs on the Lancs' engines to ensure good combustion of the petrol/air mixture. So important were they to the smooth running of the aircraft and safety of the crew, two were fitted to each engine. Both would undergo a pre-flight check by the pilot.

He did this by revving each engine and switching each of its magnetos off in turn, listening for a drop in engine revs. If the revs remained constant the magnetos were producing big fat sparks. If any of the eight magnetos were suspect, take-off was aborted and the pilot would return to his dispersal point for an electrician to run tests.

When the pilot of Charlie Delta said he had a mag drop problem and was abandoning take-off, it seemed to be a matter of common sense. You don't want a Lancaster with seven crew, ten tons of bombs and a huge quantity of fuel on board running the risk of failing at the point of take off, when the aircraft is under maximum stress. The problem in this instance was that it had happened several times before with this particular commander and subsequent diagnostic checks had revealed no faults. But by this time it would be too late to join the mission.

All flight crew had thirty missions to get in before being excused further bombing duties. It was natural they counted the days to a safe completion of their '30' so they could return to a more normal existence. If, after bracing themselves for a mission, it was abandoned, it wasn't counted towards the 30 and unhappiness followed. The same applied to the ground crew who also had the heavy work of unloading the aircraft they had just serviced. Occasional malfunctions were expected. A regular problem was indeed a problem.

In the case of Charlie Delta the pilot had lost his nerve. Everybody handles stress differently, Uncle Bill explained later. Airmen who didn't get stressed were not considered normal. Most learnt how to cope. The pilot of Charlie Delta had been unable to cope with the continuous high levels of stress with Berlin raids and Uncle Bill had to take firm action.

Pulling alongside the stationary Lancaster at the head of the runway, he leapt out, opened the fuselage door and clambered in. I sat for a minute in the mist at dusk looking down the line of remaining bombers around the perimeter. The sight and sound, the power of those machines, all engines running was awesome. The sight of two more cars without lights speeding up the runway towards us made my mind up about what I should do. Common sense suggested I shouldn't but I took Uncle Bill's earlier instruction I should stick with him and I too pulled open the fuselage door and hauled myself aboard.

Everyone seemed to be in the cockpit. The huge dark belly was empty. In front of me was the massive spar that holds the wings together. I didn't climb over it because the mêlée of shouting up front was not my business. There were some storage racks by me, like little bunks, so I climbed into the bottom one and made myself comfortable behind some stuff.

Then the door opened and two Service

Policemen scrambled in. They passed me, climbed over the spar and entered the cockpit which by now, was like Piccadilly Circus. Two minutes later they came by again, this time with a sobbing pilot. The door slammed shut behind them.

When the engines revved up to full throttle I thought we were on our way back to dispersal as quickly as possible. The aircraft bumped along for a bit and then the vibration stopped. I guessed wrong. We were airborne. I had just seen the pilot being taken off the aircraft and I climbed out of my hidey-hole and peeked towards the flight deck. The main light was off but I could clearly make out Uncle Bill by the glow of the instrument panel. My tummy heaved. I was on my way to Germany on a bombing run ...

I scrambled over the spar as quickly as I could and a hand grabbed my shoulder.

"Good God!" the Flight Engineer yelled. "Hey Skip. We've got a stowaway!"

Uncle Bill swung round and shook his head.

"You told me to stick by you," I shouted over the roar, slightly tearful since I was on the edge of big trouble, again. "I didn't know you would be taking off. We'll have to go back."

Uncle waved me forward and gestured towards the Flight Engineer's seat my discoverer had vacated. "Get your bum on that, belt up and put this on." He passed over a flying helmet and plugged it in for me. "No time for that. You'll have to stick with us, unless you want to make a parachute jump!"

He and the Flight Engineer were grinning but I

couldn't see anything funny in it. "What about Mum?"

"We can't use the radio at the moment. The Germans would hear us. She'll have to sit tight and assume you're safe. Don't worry. We'll be back long before breakfast." As I listened to Uncle Bill my nervousness faded. It was as if he was filling me up with good feelings.

"A lot of people would love to be in your situation now! We get top officers trying to get on a crew list. It's a wonderful experience. So, relax and enjoy it. I'm looking after you."

He turned away as the navigator handed him a bit of paper. After reading off some figures he reset his compass and banked gently to port. As he did the sea came into view. The light of the half-moon put a silver sheen on its surface. Ahead I could see clouds piling up far over our heads.

As we and the last half-dozen aircraft from Lindholme with us were lagging behind we could see action ahead over Holland with the forward bombers crossing the Kamhuber Line. Searchlight beams swung across the sky like lighted pencils. Dozens of anti-aircraft guns were flashing but there were no casualties. By the time we crossed, the lights had died away and the guns fallen silent. Germany lay ahead.

It was a funny feeling crossing the Rhine, unmissable once Uncle Bill pointed it out, a blue silver belt running away to the south. I knew that hundreds of other Lancasters from many other bases had joined us but couldn't see them except the nearest two occasionally in silhouette. But as long as we were all going in the same direction, there was, I thought, no need to worry.

About two hours off our target I was feeling a bit cold and a bit sleepy. At the briefing I had been nervous on the crews' behalf but it didn't feel so bad. I was quite proud of how calm I felt. Every ten minutes or so, it seemed another mug of coffee would come my way and I had to keep wending my way to the chemical toilet at the rear. When I passed the navigator he was on his toes getting a fix on the stars. The wireless operator, behind him was resting his head on his table though he had his earphones on and was no doubt hearing everything.

When I got back and plugged in again I could hear Uncle Bill chatting quietly to the crew. None of them seemed to be upset by what had happened earlier. They were sympathetic about their missing skipper and I thought this was really good. In films people can be very nasty to cowards but it wasn't like this with these guys.

"Half an hour," Uncle Bill called tersely. "Guns, watch out. Stratus at about five thousand feet, quite thick too, so ack-ack will be doing nothing but the fighters will be active."

"Keeping my eyes skinned, Skip," the rear gunner responded.

"Me too, Sir," came another.

As we droned on eastwards the yellow glow on the horizon grew. Because of the cloud, Uncle Bill explained, German anti-aircraft gunners couldn't see us, so there was no firing. But they were shining all their searchlights on the clouds so that the fighters that had come up to meet us would be able to look down and see us in silhouette.

"They," he jerked his thumb upwards, "will be hanging about at twenty thousand waiting for us to pass. So we'll have to be on our toes."

"What's that. Over there to the left?" I asked as the sky lit up for about ten seconds before dying away.

Uncle Bill turned briefly. "Their first kill." He spoke quietly. "That's the first wave being picked off."

I could feel my tummy tightening again. The relaxed feeling had drained away and my hands were sweating. It wasn't just me. There was an air of tension throughout the 'plane. No one spoke. If their mouths were as dry as mine, they wouldn't be able to.

Now the yellow glow below was the size of a lake. Beneath that lay Berlin. The searchlights didn't move. The cloud couldn't have been very thick because the brilliance was intense. I could imagine it from the fighters' view above us, watching the British bombers crawling like flies across a window. The threat of intercepting fighters was intense now and the squadron had closed up for defence. Flying Officer Cunningham's plane came along our starboard wing and I could see my friend, slouching over the controls. Looking up he gave a quick wave.

Minutes later the radio crackled into life. The Master Bomber, the 'Master of Ceremonies' for the attack in a Mosquito thousands of feet above us with, literally, a birds-eye view had also seen our arrival.

"Welcome, you chaps. Watch out for bandits. About thirty of them, after your blood. They've already knocked two out. We're using pink pansies tonight. And we're spot on. So, get on with it and get out fast."

The pink pansies were red Target Indicators on slow-drop parachutes that gave off millions of candlelights of illumination to pinpoint bomb release points. They were invaluable when, as that night, the ground couldn't be seen.

"Bomb doors open!" The bomb aimer below my legs was spreadeagled on the floor with his sight pressing against the window. Uncle Bill pulled a lever that caused a rush of air through the fuselage and the aircraft to tremble and acknowledged, "bomb doors open."

There was another burst of pink light turning night into day as another cluster of pansies ignited, thousands of feet above us. The light, bouncing off the clouds back into black space showed the bandits, like tiny pink moths peeling off on their way down to us. Cunningham, now just fifty yards away saw them too and a thumbs-up came my way.

"Fifteen seconds," the bomb aimer warned. "Keep her steady." He was the boss at that moment. "Ten seconds ..."

Cunningham was still alongside. Then I noticed movement above us, a little to the rear. Another bomber was with us, over Cunningham. Our aircraft suddenly lurched upwards.

"Bombs gone," came through the headset. And just as I heard the shout I saw bombs disgorged from our companion's belly – and from the aircraft above him also.

"Good God!" I shouted as pink-tinted bombs hurtled by us. One whipped past my window. But then a noticeably bigger bomb, a five-hundred pounder I guessed, found a premature target. It hit Cunningham's inner starboard engine, snapping his wing off as if it was a piece of celery. It didn't explode. Bombs have to fall a long way before the little windmill on their noses sets the fuse.

I watched, horrified, as the Lancaster rolled slowly over and dived. Fuel from its ruptured wing tank spewed across the fuselage, hit the remaining engines and exploded. The aircraft dropped, a ball of flame and disappeared through the clouds with its seven-man crew.

"Cunningham's gone!" I shouted in disbelief, looking over my shoulder.

"Yes," Uncle Bill responded tautly. "No fuss."

"But ..."

"No fuss, Neil," he said again, his voice cold and crisp.

"Hard a port!" someone yelled, the urgency clearing my mind like a douche. Pushing the stick forward, we dived hard left through the cloud leaving my stomach in the air and me glad I was strapped in. As we did so, a fighter, black as a bat, hurtled across us its guns blazing. It missed.

We were down to three thousand feet before we recovered and began climbing again in an arc. The whole of Berlin lay below us. The incendiaries dropped by the first wave were doing their work. Hundreds of what looked like little fires couldn't have been little, as line after line of avenues blazed across the city. In some parts, clusters of bombs had caused an inferno. It looked bad for the Berliners but we didn't wait to see.

Uncle took us back up to the safety of the cloud and there we stayed for our return to the English Channel apart from bobbing up occasionally for a star fix. The turbulence made it a rocky ride but, as uncle said, better than bumping into any fighters that might have been prowling.

Our navigator received a "well done!" over the radio as we dropped below the cloud base at four thousand feet over Spurn Head. Twenty minutes later, as the sun was climbing out of its spongy mattress of Thorne Marshes, we touched down.

Though it was dawn, Mum was up, waiting. I climbed wearily out of the aircraft with the rest of the crew.

"You never cease to amaze!" She shook her head slowly before pushing me into the car.

On the way home she told me the AOC himself had come to see her in the mess after it was clear I had gone off with Uncle Bill. He enjoined her to total silence about what had happened as there would be serious consequences for him. Although it hadn't been his fault, the upper brass at the Air Ministry wouldn't see it that way. They would expect an aircraft to turn back immediately a stowaway was discovered. The point was, he said, if the 'plane had crashed and the body of a boy had been found, Goebbels and the whole Nazi propaganda machine would have had a field day with it.

So, she said finally, "Mum's definitely the word! We won't even tell your father. A few gins in him and he would be sure to let it out!"

One hour later I was at home, in bed and asleep.

Chapter Fifteen

In the spring of 1944, I was lying on the settee at home immobilized by a large abscess on my leg. During some fooling around with my classmates at De La Salle I had fallen off one of its air raid shelters and cut myself. Dad had swathed the wound in penicillin *nonad tulle*, a pad of greeny-yellow gauze thick with grease that had penicillin in it. It was the same stuff as used on wounded soldiers.

I was enjoying doing nothing when the 'phone went. Mum rushed from the kitchen to answer it. It was David. As my brother David was in isolation hospital with diphtheria Mum, thought for a moment it was him. But no, it was her elder brother. I heard her say "this is a surprise." They didn't really keep in touch. Then there was silence. Then Mum started to howl like a wolf. She kept saying "oh, my God! No. It can't be. No David. It must be a mistake."

Dragging myself off the settee I went into the hall. Mum was sitting on the bottom step of the stairs with the 'phone clamped to her ear. As I prised it from her hand she looked up at me and said "your Uncle Bill's been killed."

She was beside herself. Ringing Dad, who was at

Totley surgery I whispered Uncle Bill been killed and held the earpiece close to Mum. She couldn't say anything but Dad got the message. Twenty minutes later he was sitting beside her on the stairs with his arm around her.

That night she got drunk. Sitting with Dad in the lounge she slurped gin after gin but it didn't have the desired effect. She kept saying "there'll be no body. He told me the Germans just put stones in the coffin. Stones ..."

Auntie Margaret arrived with Uncle Ged who had trained with Dad at Cork University. Uncle Ged had been in the army. He'd been a medical officer at Narvik in Norway and the experience had toughened him up. On one occasion with the ground frozen and so many bodies to bury, British and German, he had got grave-digging parties from the two sides working alongside each other to get the job done.

He was just the kind of person you needed in a situation like this. Dad sat baffled by the grief and did nothing but dole out gin. Uncle Ged cut through the drama with a no-nonsense approach, just like Uncle Bill's over Berlin when Cunningham's Lancaster had tumbled out of the sky.

By the time I went to bed Mum was quite garrulous and with her arms round Margaret sat chewing over the 'old days' when they were kids.

With most deaths during the war was there was no body and all the normal business of hymns and a funeral was not possible. This meant no real closure. There were many womenfolk who, long after their men had been killed, still ran to the door whenever the bell rang convinced it was all a mistake and that the missing man would walk in with a smile, his kit bag over his shoulder. Hundreds of thousands of soldiers lost their lives and the 'papers often wrote about such instances.

I think Mum was like this for a long time. Every time the 'phone went she would start up and because the surgery had a lot calls, it might happen dozens of times a day. She didn't say so, of course. But I knew from the look on her face she still hoped for the news she wanted to hear. It became a part of her life.

My sympathy soon faded. Kids are more self-centred and have too much new ahead of them to carry these sadnesses for long. We just left her to it.

Three weeks afterwards at the beginning of June, Michael and I went camping. We were with the 203rd Sheffield Scout Troop and as Whit Weekend was starting, we met at Millhouses Station and set off down the Hope Valley south-west of Sheffield. The government weren't keen on this sort of thing. German planes were still making sorties across the North Sea and tents in fields were a temptation. It had happened a lot.

Every time we walked to Scouts we passed a garage with a large car in the forecourt that had been machine-gunned on a country lane nearby. The inside of the vehicle was spattered with dried blood and what looked like black, mincemeaty bits of body. We thought it was really exciting and had a competition to count the number of bullet holes. I reckoned it was forty-four but Micheal came up with nearly sixty.

The problem was, some of the bullets – these were machine gun, not cannon – had passed right through the car and you had to look at how the metal around the holes was bent to decide whether it was an 'inner' or an 'outer.' From the number of holes we believed the aircraft must have made several passes to get the results it did.

But, whether we were to be machine-gunned or not it was fun to get away. We went off on hikes and had meals that were generally awful as they were made from dried egg, dried milk and corned beef or Spam. The main exercise was building a rope bridge over a stream. The rule was we had to use three kinds of knots, bowline, sheepshank and I can't remember the third because I thought knots were silly. Our Scoutmaster didn't and we had to do and undo them many times until he was satisfied.

As soon as the sun set we had to put out our fire because of blackout regulations and did this by standing around peeing on the burning embers, sending up clouds of smelly steam.

When we got up on the second day our campsite field was littered with silvery aluminium strips about half an inch wide and nine inches long. Nervous they were some kind of German weapon our Troop Leader made us gather them up and after stuffing them in bags we made for Hope Police Station. Our arrival excited no interest. The sergeant, after a brief inspection, announced it to be stuff dropped by the

RAF. He didn't know what they were but they were certainly not German.

Putting them in his bin he thanked us for our interest and then asked if we were the silly buggers who had been knocking down the dry stone walls. These walls, it seems, took a very long time to build and as they prevented sheep from wandering they were important to national security. War Agricultural Committee Inspectors were looking for the culprits so if it was us we should go back and build them up again or we could find ourselves in poky! In the end however, in the face of our Troop Leader's passionate denial that Boy Scouts would ever be so irresponsible, he let us go.

When we got back home, there was a flap on. The Second Front they called D-Day had started. It was something everyone had been expecting as there were American soldiers everywhere. I used to go up to them in town and deliver the magic words "any gum, chum?" to be rewarded with a small green packet of the stuff. On one occasion the GI I approached responded haughtily "I'm an officer!" and swept past.

The Daily Mail had maps on their front page and Michael and I would cut them out and stick them on our bedroom wall. We knew all about Caen, Villers-Bocage and this Falaise Gap through which the Germans were trying to escape and how General Montgomery and General Patton had trapped them and blasted them to pieces.

Uncle Bill had been heavily involved in the preparations for the Normandy landings that began just four weeks after his death. Soon after this, Doodlebugs made an appearance over London. These were like little aeroplanes but they were powered by a jet engine with no pilot. The BBC put a recording of their noise on the news. First you would hear a loud, stuttering drone, like a very big bee suffering from a cold. Then there would be a sudden silence followed after about 15 seconds by an almighty bang. These were a new menace for Londoners, though they knew if one passed over with its engine still running, they were safe.

We didn't worry about them because they only had a range of 150 miles so they couldn't come anywhere near Sheffield. But we were wrong. On Christmas Eve 1944 we found out just how wrong we were. I was fast asleep in my bunk bed when I heard Michael jump up and run to the window. Opening the curtains he stared out. Dragging myself up I stood beside him.

"Look!" he pointed.

As I followed his finger I could see a bright flame coming up from Norton. It was about five hundred feet up in the sky and heading in our direction. Then I heard the drone. There was no doubt about what it was. And to confirm it the sirens suddenly started howling. My legs turned to jelly. Rushing back to my bunk I squirmed into the little gap under it and put a pillow over my head.

Michael was much braver. He didn't move. As I lay in a funk he carried on a running commentary as the droning turned into a roar. "It's here," he yelled finally. And it made the floor tremble under me. As

I was thinking of screaming, it passed over. Its droning then faded and there was silence and we couldn't be sure its engine had not cut-out, though there was no explosion.

"It passed straight over us!" Michael was really excited.

I heard Dad open his bedroom door. As he came into our room I could feel wet running down my legs and breathed a sigh of relief that Clare wasn't here. But I could hear her voice "Jesus Christ, Niall, you're pissing yourself ..." Dragging off my pyjama trousers I slunk back into bed. Mum found them in the morning when she came to call us but didn't say a word. Not a single word.

The following morning the news was full of it. The government had been surprised at the targeting of Sheffield and good old Manchester, it seems but the mystery had been solved by a fisherman who had been out on his boat offshore from Mablethorpe. He said a number of German aircraft, subsequently identified as Heinkel IIs, had flown over from the continent carrying the Doodlebugs under their bellys. As soon as they had reached our shore they had released them.

Few of them reached Manchester, ending up mostly on the Pennine moors. Nobody had been hurt but my self-esteem had taken a battering. Boys of twelve were expected to be brave and not skulk under bunks wetting themselves. So I decided that from now on I would be braver. Maybe not as brave as Uncle Bill but a bit more like him.

The following morning I got out my atlas and

drew a line from Mablethorpe to our house. Then I continued it on to the moors and was convinced it had come down at Ringinglow. Packing my haversack I told Mum I was going hiking. Catching the bus I went into Sheffield bus station and caught another to Ringinglow. I got there about eleven o'clock.

The moors never look good in winter. They look sort of sullen, as though they don't want to be there either. They stretched, as in the hymn we used to sing at Mass "o'er moor and fen, o'er crag and torrent till, the night is gone."

In many ways they frightened me. They were so lonely you knew if you went out on your own and something went wrong, like you broke your leg or got stuck in a bog, you were finished. There was nobody to hear your shouting. And, if you stumbled around you could end up drowning in the wet, peaty ground.

As I got off the bus a cold wind was blowing. Rain was spattering and mist drifted like curtains dragged by the wind but I was determined to be brave and set off walking.

I plodded for about three miles over the fells and it was just as my bravery was fading and my boots were filling with water I heard voices. I couldn't see anything but as I clambered round a big lump of Millstone Grit sticking up from the peat I saw them, three Home Guards. Hunched down in the heather they were sheltering from the wind. They'd got a little fire going and were sitting round it rubbing their hands. Beside them their rifles were locked in a pyramid.

"Hey there, young man!" One of the men with two corporal's stripes stood up. "Bugger off ..." The other two looked at me casually and then huddled further down sucking on cigarettes.

"What's happening?"

"Never mind what's happening. It's secret. Bugger off!"

About a hundred yards beyond him I could see a black ring where the growth had been burned away and some jagged bits of metal sticking up.

"It's that Doodlebug, isn't it?"

"Doodlebug?"

"The one that passed over my house last night. I'm tracking its path!"

The man shrugged his shoulders and sat down again. "If you know, then everyone knows. It's no secret then."

"Can I have a look at it?"

"No, the Captain's on his way and if he sees you here we're for it."

One of them called out "leave 'im alone Corp. It's gone off now so he can't come to any hurt."

"What's that?" I pointed to a large pile of heather and bracken that had been freshly pulled up. "Is there a body under there?"

"Body? Ay!" Going over, the corporal pulled the bracken open. A cloud of feathers wafted out and floated away in the wind. There were bodies, lots of them. Grouse and pheasant by the bucket load. As I moved closer one of the privates came across.

"A hundred and twenty. A hundred and bleedin'

twenty!" he said. "Those Jerries are the cause. Place is thick with game birds. There's been no shooting since the war started. Breeding like rabbits. All the toffs are off in France or somewhere, so they have the place to themselves. No nasty 12-bore to interrupt their peaceful lives. And then comes this bleeding bomb. Slaughter. Bloody slaughter."

He looked around and asked quietly, "got any money?"

"A postal order for five bob."

Mum had given me the money to buy one to send to Clare for Christmas but as I had no inclination to be kind to her after what she had done to me, I hadn't sent it.

"Corp," my new friend shouted across to the grumpy man who had sunk back into the heather, "he's got five bob. Shall I give him some?"

A head popped up. "'E can 'ave the whole bloody lot for me. Officers'll only take 'em."

"You can sell them when you get home, lad. Get you half a dollar apiece. Give us your money then. And hurry up, Captain could be here soon."

Handing over my postal order I opened my haversack and took out my sandwiches which I shared out. Then, with the soldiers helping, I stuffed bird after bird back in their place. It was quite a big bag so we managed to get twenty-six in. At half a crown each that would be over three pounds. I could swap my bike for a new one with three pounds. Pulling the straps tight, they lifted the haversack up and put it on my back.

"Off you go now, mate. Quick. Don't want the

Captain to see you. If you see an officer, go off in the other direction."

But I didn't see any officer. After a brief examination of the remains of the Doodlebug I trudged back to the bus terminus.

There was a bus waiting. Its driver and conductor were standing on the reversing road having a fag before starting off and they stood and gazed as I walked up.

"Been doing a bit of poaching then?"

"No."

"Tha's covered in feathers, lad. And I can see a wing coming out of tha' bag. Can we have one then? It's Christmas tomorrow and it'll be Spam roll for the both of us otherwise!"

"I'm sure he'll want to be nice to us," the other one confirmed with an edge to his voice. "A nice present."

I took a deep breath. If they stopped by the police station I could lose the lot. They were blackmailing me. If I didn't get on their bus it would be a twenty-mile walk. Dropping my bag I pulled out two of my birds and handed them one each.

"Tha'rt a good lad," the conductor grinned. "And we'll charge thi' nowt for takin' thi' back to Sheffield!"

"Tha' wants to keep them better hid than that though if tha's going through town. Here ..." The driver and his mate laid in to my bag and after a lot of pushing and pulling got it neat and tidy. Then off we went.

I'd decided to do my hawking on James Andrew

Crescent. The houses looked very posh there and I felt they would be keen to have an addition to their pork chops which, as far as I could see, would be the main Christmas dinner for that year. I was right. Within half an hour I'd sold twenty-one birds. The bus people had two. That made twenty-three. The remaining three would be for Mum.

As I came down the Crescent onto Greenhill Main Road there was a policeman standing outside the ARP centre, where the air raid wardens gathered when they weren't digging people out of wrecked buildings or bellowing "put that light out!" and threatening to take you to court if you didn't. The policeman looked hard at me. Then, just when I reached the bottom by Greenhill Main Road he crooked his finger.

"Me?" I pointed to myself.

"You!" was the gruff response. He pointed to my bag as I approached. "Show me."

"Show you what?"

He rocked on his heels for a moment. "It'll be Christmas Day soon. In ..." he pulled his fob watch out, " ... about six hours. Don't want to be hanging about 'till then do we?"

I opened my bag and held it up for inspection. Fumbling through it he pulled out my three remaining victims of the Doodlebug. "Nice fat ones aren't they!" Resting his cape on the wall he laid the little corpses carefully by it.

"They were killed by that Doodlebug. I've just come back from Ringinglow."

"So they're Government property then?"

"What?"

"Died as a result of enemy action. Mister Churchill has to be compensated. His property then aren't they?"

"I ... er suppose so."

"Suppose, suppose? There's no supposing about it." Unfolding his cape he laid the birds carefully along its length, rolled it up again and arranged the bulge at the top end. Lifting it back onto his shoulder he adjusted it until it was comfortable. Then he fixed me with a gimlet stare. "Aren't you going to say thank you?"

"Why?" I was beginning to feel mad.

"Why?" He affected an air of disbelief. "You ask me why?" He pointed to my pocket. "How much money have you made out of this unfortunate episode?"

"Going on for three pounds."

"And what is a lad like you going to do with three pounds?"

"Swap my bike. I want a better bike."

"There, you see." He patted me on the shoulder. "So now you can have a bike. A better bike. I'm Father Christmas and I'm letting you have all that money you've purloined from Mister Churchill for a bike. Isn't that kind of me?"

Turning round he ambled off towards Four Lane Ends leaving me scratching my head.

After the Christmas of 1944 everyone was aware things were drawing to a close. 'If' soon became 'when'. Michael and I kept our maps up-to-date. The

Russians had given the Germans a pasting in the summer in their Operation Bagration that was even bigger than D-Day and were pushing ever closer to Berlin. Our armies, led by Patton and Montgomery were falling behind in the race but a lot of people were saying their boss, General Eisenhower didn't want to get there first because he wanted the Russians to do all the hard work. Then we saw Mussolini, Hitler's pal in charge of Italy, hanged from a garage roof and planning for bonfires and other celebrations started. Mum started making flags ready to hang out of our upstairs windows.

When the end did finally arrive it wasn't as exciting as I expected. I think we had been building up to it for so long it just went a bit flat. But celebrations had to go ahead. A massive bonfire had been set in a football field in the middle of the Greenhill Estate. Because it was a council estate Mum didn't like us going there. She thought they weren't our sort of people.

I thought maybe it was a good thing, them being different from us. Those folk who Mum thought were our sort of people were not always very interesting. They were generally doctors' families or the owners of big city shops or, like Mr. Rumble or Uncle David, little mesters. Most of their kids went to boarding schools and stuck their noses up at kids who went to ordinary schools. They were boring.

Most of their daughters were highfalutin' and wore bottle green knickers which went down to their knees. Some of them were like Clare. If they caught you looking they would whisper to their friends and laugh. Their mothers used to sit around talking about clothes and if you went near their girls they would wag their fingers and say "no hanky-panky!"

The kind of people who lived on the Greenhill Council Estate were quite nice when you got to know them although they did eat a lot of fish and chips. I got friendly with Geoff. He was a blacksmith and his forge was in an old house on the edge of the estate. He always kept the forge window open because it got very hot and I used to go and lean on the window and watch him work. He didn't make horseshoes like you'd expect of a blacksmith because horses hadn't been used much in this war, not in Britain. And the government wouldn't allow him the iron anyway. He made parts for tanks. It wasn't for Shermans, as they were made in America, but for Matildas which everyone said were rubbish.

I had a friend whose uncle was in a Matilda on the Second Front and his tank was blown to pieces killing everyone apart from him. This was because the armour was so thin, he said. They used to say "never fart at Matilda because the lady will fart back and blow your arse off."

Geoff used to work in a singlet and shorts. He had a lot of muscles from banging away with his hammer. He was really friendly and I used to go shooting with him on the moors. He was so brilliant he could shoot a rabbit's head off at fifty yards with a 12-bore shotgun. He explained that shooting heads off was a good idea because it kept the pellets away from the meat. He tried to show me how to do it but I was a dead loss. At any rate I didn't like the bangs because they gave me a headache. So I used to stand behind him and just watch.

At Greenhill we had a maid called Gwen. She seemed to be a bit simple so Mum got her for a pound a week. Sometimes she would take the kids out walking and sometimes I would go with her. If I suggested we went down Annesley Road, where the council estate started, she always thought it a good idea. And if I suggested we stop at Geoff's forge and have a chat with him well, that was a good idea too.

The kids even enjoyed it because they could go in and look at the furnace and watch the sparks shooting up as Geoff hit the iron. So we would stay for hours. And Mum thought it was a good idea because it kept us from being under her feet. She didn't, of course, know we had gone into the estate and only found out when David came home with his new jumper which had cost ten points and you couldn't get clothes without points. Well, David's new jumper had a rash of little burn holes in it from where the sparks had landed and Mum went mad and told us next time we went walking we had to go down Hemper Lane. They were private houses and they weren't the kind of people who burned holes in little boys' jumpers.

Gwen put a sulky face on when she said that. But on her day off she still used to go and see Geoff. I know because I would sometimes pass them on the way home from school. I told her I would tell Mum what she was doing. But she said she would give me a big kiss to keep my mouth shut. So when Mum and Dad went out on a Thursday night, which they always did, she got the kids off to bed and then took me into the lounge and gave me a big kiss. I really enjoyed it. But when my hand fell onto her knee she jumped up and gave me a slap. But the next Thursday I got another kiss but, before giving it, she warned me if I let my hands roam again there would be no more kisses. So I stuck to the bargain. But next time I called at Geoff's forge I saw her sitting with him having a cup of tea and his hand was on her knee. But she wasn't slapping him.

Mum and Dad went out on VE night as they were calling it. There was to be a big celebration at the golf club and Mum said that as they wouldn't be back 'till late, Gwen had to make sure we were in bed by eleven o'clock.

As soon as they had gone, Gwen said she wanted a little favour. She wanted Geoff to visit and if I agreed not to tell Mum I could have an extra kiss. I declined the kiss not because I was bored with them but because I wanted something more. I wanted to go to the big bonfire down Annesley Road and for her not to tell Mum.

So it was agreed. She said Geoff would lock the drive gate so that if they came back early they'd have to blow the horn. She would tell them it had been done because of all the drunks around. If Geoff heard them honking he could nip over the wall into next door.

I could suit myself and her lips would stay sealed. The carnival spirit filling the Greenhill Estate was infectious. At first I felt a bit self-conscious entering what, in Mum's eyes, was 'enemy territory'. But it was unnecessary. The street lights were full on and the gloom of the 'dim out', the successor to the 'black out' had disappeared. Instead of huddling indoors, as they had done for five years, everyone was out. The streets were flooded with cheerful, chattering people of all ages. It seemed to me like the first day of a Spring that was never going to fade.

There were a lot of soldiers around. The de-mobbing as it was known, had started as soon as we had crossed the German borders and although some soldiers were due to go to the Pacific, that felt different. It was the Germans that had been the real enemy. They had reduced the centre of Sheffield to rubble and dragged people out of bed night after night with the threat of blowing their homes to fragments. It was they who had run those horrible camps we had seen on the news. And now they had been crushed.

Bad as the Japanese war was, it had never got under the skin of everyone in the way the German one had. It was too remote. It was, callously, seen as the Yanks' War and we, unfairly dismissing their gigantic effort to free Europe, were leaving it to them. We had done our whack and would optimistically, reap the rewards.

Sheffield Council had supplied most of the wood for the bonfire from the wreckings caused by the German air raids. It was enormous and as the barrels of paraffin burst into flames, the wood caught, rearing up to lick at the stars and send a blast of heat across to soften the shivers of that May evening.

There was a brass band. 'God Save the Queen' challenged 'Rule Britannia' and 'There'll Always be an England' in setting the mood of the evening before continuing with 'White Cliffs of Dover', 'It's a Lovely Day Tomorrow', 'Roll Out the Barrel', 'Silver Wings in the Moonlight' and a host of similar tunes that everyone applied their voices to with such enthusiasm you couldn't hear yourself think. But nobody wanted to think. There'd been enough of that done through the war and now it was fun, fun, fun.

All the ladies kissed me and I kissed all the ladies offering. I knew history was happening and I was determined to have a part in it. By about ten o'clock the real fun got going. The band, well refreshed with beer began with great gusto 'Roll Me Over, Lay Me Down and Do It Again'.

"This is number three and his hand is on my knee. Roll me over lay me down and do it again. Roll me over in the clover, roll me over lay me down and do it again."

"Now we're at number six he's doing tricks. Roll me over ... now we're at number eight he bent me over the garden gate ... now we're at number nine and the baby's doing fine ... at number ten when he's done we'll do it again ..."

Soon, couples were on the grass, clothes were being removed and older people were departing, grim-faced, dragging their kids with them.

"Would you like to roll me over?" A hand caught mine and I turned to see a girl with lank blonde hair smiling up at me. "You are tall aren't you? Are you enjoying it?"

She moved closer and pressed herself into me. "My name's Sylvia, what's yours?"

"Neil," I swallowed.

"Well, Neil," she squeezed my hand, "I only live across the road. Would you like to come across?"

"Can't we stay here a bit longer?"

She shook her head. "I've got a baby and my sitter's going home."

"Er ..."

By now I was feeling stupid. Erroll Flynn was one of my idols, particularly in the way he bowled women over. He would have sneered at the way I was handling this situation, tongue-tied, indecisive, terrified.

"Come on," she said gently, leading me out of the field. She stopped on the pavement. "Have you any French Letters? You do want to, don't you?"

"Well, I er ..."

"Nip up to that house on the corner. The lady there is a midwife. She'll help you. I'll be waiting!" She disappeared down the gennel between the two semis. Heart thumping I went up to the midwife's and knocked gently on the door.

"That lady from ..."

"At it again, is she?" the midwife tutted, lifting a purple and white packet off the hall window ledge.

"Have you got a half-crown?"

I pulled the money out and handed it over.

"You seem a nice lad. Be kind to her." With that she slammed the door.

The band had packed in now and the field was emptying. Feeling as if I was in a dream I went up the gennel and through the door being held open. Grabbing hold of me, Sylvia gave me a hug then undid my jacket. "Go into the back room. I'm just going up to change. Back in a minute."

The back room was a bit sparse. A battered-looking settee, a pram and a table half-covered with pots was all there was. I could hear Sylvia moving around upstairs. Putting the precious packet on the table I took my shirt off. I wasn't quite sure how I would handle this, or the French Letters. But then, as she seemed to be doing all the handling, I would leave it to her. Slipping my trousers off I lay back on the settee. Then I heard the baby cry. Coming halfway down the stairs she called for me pass up the bottle on the table.

"Oo ..." she smiled looking at my bare legs, "you are making yourself comfortable! I'll be down in a minute."

Returning to the settee I laid down and closed my eyes. I was just nodding off when I heard some shuffling outside. Then there was a bang as the back door flew open. In came a soldier with a kit bag and rifle over his shoulder. He propped his gun against the wall in the back room, saw me and said "who the fuck are you?"

I went completely cold. All I could see was the paratrooper's badge on his breast a well-Blancoed lance corporal's stripe and a grizzled, angry face.

Coming forward he grabbed me by my shoulders, hauled me to my feet and repeated, "who the fuck are you?" Spittle on his lips flew into my face.

"I'm Neil. I'm ..."

There was a scream.

"Alfie!" Sylvia, in her dressing gown, wrapped her arms round the soldier. "Why didn't you let me know?"

"Letter's obviously not reached you yet." Squeezing her tight he lifted her up and gave her a kiss. Letting out a moan she said, "I've been waiting for you. Oh, it's so lovely darling."

"And if it's so fucking lovely then who's this?" He nodded towards me.

"Oh, him." She paused. "It's our Charlotte's boyfriend. They had a row. I'm letting him kip for the night. He's only a kid."

Alfie stared me up. "It's not the length of the gun but the strength of the powder that matters, eh?" he sniggered. "Your Charlotte's a rum 'un. How old are you kid?"

"Fifteen."

"If you're fifteen I'm Adolf Bloody 'Itler, you lying little bugger."

"He'll be gone in the morning." She embraced Alfie again and looking at me over his shoulder, rolled her eyes.

"Oh, yes?" Pushing her away he picked up the unopened Durex packet. "A nightcap, is it?"

Lifting them out of his hand, Sylvia looked at them and turned on me. "You dirty little bastard. What are these for? There's no Charlotte here for your dirty little plans. So were you planning to creep up on me during the night?"

"Er ..."

"He looks that type, doesn't he, Sylvy? Smarmy. I'm surprised you let him in the house. Should have seen. Well ..." he picked up my clothes and stomping to the door, slung them into the street, " ... he's not stopping here. We've got things to do! And you, you little bastard," he smashed his fist into my face, "can get out now ..."

I spent the night huddled by the dying bonfire feeling really sorry for myself. I didn't want to go home in case I woke anyone. As dawn broke I saw others still in the field, singles and couples. Pulling myself up I crossed the road and tiptoed up the tunnel to Sylvia's front door. There was no sound and I sat down and waited. After maybe an hour the wailing of a baby filtered through the thin wood. I reckoned that Alfie wouldn't be up looking after it. And I was right. I tapped cautiously on the door and was relieved it was Sylvia who opened it.

"You!" her eyes widened. Pulling her dressing gown closed she tied the sash. "Come in. Don't worry, he's out for the count, brought a bottle of whisky with him and drank the lot."

I followed her to the back room. She picked up the baby from the settee and lowered it into its pram.

"So, what can I do for you?" she asked coyly. She didn't look very good. Her eyes were bleary and her make-up had smudged. She took a hanky from her pocket, licked it and came towards my face with it, looking a bit concerned. I backed off.

"Can I have my French Letters back, please? I want to get my money back."

She raised her eyebrows. "Brave little bugger aren't you? Not quite Errol Flynn, is it!" She sat on the settee for a moment in a thoughtful silence disturbed only by the baby's breathing.

"We had a busy time last night. But that needn't stop you." She stood up, caught my hand and pulled me gently towards her. "They're all gone but ... you know what to do."

Well, I didn't know what to do. And I was too tired to care. She got the message and it was her turn to back off. Lifting a bag from the settee she fiddled in her purse and found half a crown. She pressed it into my hand. "Here. It's yours."

Thanking her, I turned to the door.

"But, half a mo', Neil." She caught my hand again. "He's not been demobbed. It's embarkation leave, just for a week. He'll be gone Wednesday, to Malaya."

She gave me a look that made me go weak at the knees. "It's your first time, isn't it?"

I didn't need to answer.

"If you want to come back make it a night, any night after Wednesday. And don't worry about ... supplies."

She pecked me on the cheek and opened the door. As I stepped out into the morning there was a roar from upstairs. "Tea, Sylvy. I'm bloody parched!" She gave me a little smile and I smiled back and I was glad I had found the courage to call back.

Mum was in a bad way when I got in and didn't even ask where I had been. The golf club celebration had gone on until dawn, then Dad had been called out by a midwife at about five. Turning from the sink she stared bleary-eyed.

"That's a shiner!"

She went and fetched a jar of ointment from the dispensary and rubbed it gently around my eye. She poured a bowl of cornflakes out for me, put sugar and milk on the table and picking up the paper announced she was going back to bed. Looking back from the kitchen doorway she said,

"It's been a long war hasn't it, Neil?"

She closed the door behind her and I listened to her treading gently up the stairs. I suppose it was. I didn't know anything else.

Epilogue

Uncle Bill had everything going for him. He was strikingly handsome and had a calm authoritative manner. He was a Commanding Officer. Perhaps most important of all, he was a hero. It was not one Distinguished Flying Cross he was awarded; a silver rose embedded in the ribbon showed he won it twice.

He was also a caring uncle and good friend to me and the family. When I was ill he flew to Ireland to comfort me. When I was terrified over Berlin he helped me get a grip on myself. He was also, as the situation required, a Dutch Uncle, always fair in his criticism or admonishment.

He was in fact, a perfect role model for me moving from childhood into adolescence. It is not the easiest time in one's life and to add to this kid's problems there was a full-blown war going on, separation, sickness, death and assorted other tragedies and dramas all around.

Young Bill went up to Cambridge. He was a rowing Blue and after graduating in engineering went to Canada. He also joined the RAF as a weekend pilot while at Cambridge and after passing out of RAF Brough was gazetted as a Pilot Officer in the Voluntary Reserve committed to returning to uniform in the event of war.

In the early stages of the war and having re-trained on the more sophisticated aircraft that had replaced those in which he got his wings in the 1930s, he went on sorties against the battle cruisers Gneisenau and Scharnhorst in Brest in the middle of 1941 for repairs. He also did a number of 'market gardening' runs, leaflet drops. All of his sorties were accomplished without injury due, his crews said, to scrupulous care in planning raids and reviewing their results on return.

During 1941 he was promoted to Flight Lieutenant and moved to Finningley near Doncaster as Chief Flying Instructor. Here he picked up his first DFC and the extra stripe of a Squadron Leader. In the middle of 1942 uncle, now Wing Commander of 50 Squadron at RAF Swinderby completed his first operation in a Lancaster to Genoa. During 1942 and 1943 he went on to complete numerous raids over Germany, including many to Berlin. He married in 1943 and moved from 50 Squadron to head aircrew 1654 Conversion Unit at RAF Wigsley where pilots clocked up hours on the heavy bombers, Lancasters and Halifaxes.

By the beginning of 1944 he had added a bar to his DFC and completed almost fifty sorties. This was an extraordinarily high number. With an average of four per cent aircraft losses per raid, a simple calculation shows that completing one tour of thirty sorties was dangerous enough with a statistical one hundred and twenty per cent loss of aircraft. Reality bore this out. In the mess halls and bars of RAF stations there was a constant changing of personnel. There were special squads for bagging up and the discrete removal of the personal effects of aircrew that would not be coming back.

As a Commanding Officer, uncle had the job of writing the letters of condolence, sometimes as many as thirty after a heavy raid. He took great care over them. If he hadn't actually known the person he would talk to their friends and colleagues before writing. Even then, the task was a difficult one as sometimes a new arrival had not even unpacked his bag, or even slept in the bed allocated to him before the mission from which he would not return.

In February 1944 he transferred to RAF Tempsford, an airfield renowned for its very high casualty rates. This was the base from which contact with Resistance groups in occupied Europe from the Arctic Circle to Africa was maintained. Day after day, aircraft of all types took off to deliver equipment, supplies and agents to these groups under the noses of the *Wehrmacht* and *Gestapo*. Operations was run largely by the Special Operations Executive in Baker Street, London. Some claim the SOE was run by bumbling amateurs. Others say it made a major contribution in denting the formidable German war machine. The argument still rages.

What is known is that the SOE had been compromised. Many agents and aircrew had been killed by German intelligence who had themselves arranged with Baker Street exact times and places of who and what was to be dropped. Aircrews at Tempsford did their job in as professional a manner as any other RAF squadron. It included the added danger of low-level – some say suicidal – flying at 500 feet staying beneath radar and facilitating accuracy when dropping supplies.

Into this bubbling cauldron came Uncle Bill. He was involved immediately with Operation Citronelle, the supporting and co-ordinating of efforts by the Ardennes' *Maquis* to hinder German military movement towards Normandy once D-Day had commenced. It was not known that almost all its wireless operators were by then working with a Luger pointing at the back of their heads.

On the evening of May 7, uncle took off from Tempsford in Halifax LL 280 of 138 Squadron on his thirteenth mission with Citronelle and sixtieth overall. In addition to dropping equipment at Charleville-Mézières near the French-Belgian border in the southern Ardennes they were to drop an agent into a clearing in woods at Saint Denis d'Orque, a village a few kilometres west of Le Mans. All such missions were important, this one important enough to have scheduled two drops on a May night with the second leg being an incredibly dangerous journey around Paris with dawn lighting the sky.

At the same time as they were approaching Le Mans from the north-east, a Messerschmitt Bf 110 from Amiens airfield was on a convergent course. Passing over Le Mans this formidable two-seater fighter-bomber equipped with radar for night operation turned west towards Saint Denis d'Orques. After circling it moved over the extensive wooded area north of the village, the *Forêt De La Grand Charnie*, where it continued to circle.

On the ground at a farm three kilometres or so south of the village a young farmer's son, Gaston Cormier, was woken by the aircraft circling in darkness. Like many boys he was keen on aircraft recognition and knew by the slightly discordant sound, the aircraft was a twin-engined Messerschmitt fighter. It was waiting for something.

The eastern horizon was brightening as the fighter pilot picked up the approaching Halifax on radar. He would have swung in a wide arc to come up behind his target. Below them a convoy of German lorries and armoured cars debouched from barracks at Le Mans was also on its way to the village. They didn't want to arrive on the scene too early, as the *Maquis* waiting for its *rendezvous* with the Halifax would warn the British pilot of their presence. The trap was baited.

Gaston and his brother Robert got up and stood by

the window. They had heard an approaching British bomber and like the Estivals' *Maquis* in the surrounding woods, they waited. The end was swift. Gaston described the Halifax catching fire after a burst of machine-gun fire from the rear at close-quarters and of an explosion on the aircraft before it passed through a stand of poplar trees 200 metres from the farm, snapping their trunks and crash-landing in a field. The fighter roared triumphantly over its kill.

A group of men, six or seven, the boys remember, ran onto the field, opened the door of the burning wreckage and brought one man out alive. They took him to one of their father's barns but he died almost immediately from his burns.

The *Maquis* disappeared and the Germans arrived minutes later. "They behaved like mad things", Gaston remembers, driving round and round the fields looking for escapers and ruining the new crops. They soon found the one in the barn. A local woman had tried to give him wine. The rest of the crew, including uncle, were found piled up in the burnt-out cockpit, the force of the landing having catapulted them forward. They had not survived.

After the war the graves, which are in Le Mans' *Cimetière de L'Ouest*, were exhumed by the RAF's No. 1 Missing Research and Enquiry Unit and the bodies formally identified. They confirmed an eighth body, as well as those of the seven crew members, as did the Imperial War Graves Commission in 1951. Mother's belief that the Germans filled airman's coffins with stones was false. All the paperwork done by them was scrupulously correct. The agent may or may not have been a woman, since *Monsieur* Cormier retrieved a woman's shoe from a corner of the navigator's desk after the Germans had removed the bodies. This mystery remains.

Uncle, with his crew, no doubt his friends also are interred in three single and one collective grave in the Le Mans' cemetery.

F/O James Armour DFC, DFM (22) from East Acton, London.

F/O Donald Brown DFC (23) from Harborne, Birmingham, who left a wife, Mary.

F/O Alexander Bryce (25) from Edinburgh, Scotland, who left a wife, Jeanie.

F/O George Cable DFM (23) from Leeds, Yorkshire.

F/O Bernard McGonagle DFC (21) from Eltham, London.

W/Cdr William Russell DFC, Bar (35 years old) from Sheffield, Yorkshire who left a wife, Mary.

F/O Norman Sinister DFM (32) from Stalybridge, Cheshire who left a wife, Nora.

Agent unknown.

On Uncle Bill's headstone are the words: 'For they have paid all that man can owe and therefore are set free'.

Author's Notes

CHAPTER ONE
Gas Masks

During the Great War, mustard and other types of gas was used with devastating consequences on the Western front. Although the Germans were pilloried for being the first to introduce such barbaric technology into war the British and French soon followed. Civilian gas masks issued during both world wars contained asbestos and chrome and were, in the light of modern knowledge, dangerous to use. The main neutralizing agent, activated charcoal, ceased to be useful after a couple of hours.

The Sheffield Blitz began at seven o'clock on the evening of Thursday, December 12th, 1940 and lasted until four o'clock the following morning. Had gas been used the Germans couldn't have picked a better night. There was no wind and it would have pooled in the Sheaf Valley, a densely-populated area from Sharrow through to the Wicker Arches. After about nine that evening the masks would have ceased being effective and over a distance of about three miles an estimated 100,000 people might have died. And died horribly. My family were right in the middle of the area.

Hitler refrained from using gas, confident that Britain would never make the first move. Providentially, the gas masks issued in 1939 were never called into use.

CHAPTER TWO
Torpedo Attacks

The predecessor of the Leinster that I had travelled to Ireland on in 1939 was the RMS Leinster that ran a mail and passenger service between Kingstown (now Dun Laoghaire) and Holyhead. On 10 October 1918, twelve miles out from Dun Laoghaire she was struck by two torpedoes from U-boat UB-123. With 501 people of many nationalities, mostly military personnel, lost it was the greatest maritime disaster in Irish waters. There were 270 survivors. The incident provoked outrage at a time of exploratory peace talks for the ending of the Great War.

The SS Athenia, referred to by the German captain that stopped us on the way to Dublin, was sunk by a single torpedo on 3 September 1939, 250 miles off the north-west coast of Ireland. One hundred and seventeen people, of whom 28 were American and several were children perished. She was the first British ship to be sunk in WWII. Hitler condoned the cover-up and Nazi propaganda blamed Churchill for the sinking as a way of turning neutral, ie, American opinion against Germany. Many people, including Herbert Hoover did not believe the Germans could make such a blunder.

It was only during the Nuremberg Trials in 1946 that Dönitz admitted the ship had been sunk in error by U-30 and a cover-up attempted. Never fully explored is the suggestion from visible radio equipment and her erratic behaviour at sea, without identification lights, that the Athenia was involved in naval intelligence gathering.

CHAPTER FIVE
The Easter Rebellion

A large number of Irish patriots known as the Irish

Republican Brotherhood, disaffected with English rule and ceaseless discussions about Irish Home Rule, invaded the General Post Office on O'Connell Street (then Sackville Street) in the centre of Dublin and turned it into an armed fortress. After bombardment from British heavy guns, the building was set ablaze and surrender inevitably followed. The insurgents had little support from their own people at the time but when, with the support of Asquith, the British Prime Minister, the chief rebels were executed, romantic Irish hearts were stung to fury and the rest, as they say, is history.

CHAPTER SIX
Tomas Og

He was caught and sent to be hanged for the murder of *Garda* John Roche. De Valera, perhaps haunted by memories of the Troubles and of his old comrades, relented. His sentence was commuted to life imprisonment, provoking much anger at the time. After seven years he was back pacing the streets of Cork. He died, something of a folk hero, in 1994.

Hadji Beys (Hadji Bey Cie), didn't go bankrupt as a consequence of its grave loss of stock. They are still trading today.

CHAPTER NINE
Submarines

The position with regard to the use of Irish refuges by German submarines during WWII is complex. At the time of the 1922 Treaty, which gave Eire independence in the guise of calling it the Irish Free State, Michael Collins, the Irish negotiator, agreed that Cork Harbour, Beerhaven and Lough Swilly (the Treaty Ports) would be made available for use by the Royal Navy in the event of war, thus cutting a very valuable four hundred miles off the journey from the Clyde or the Mersey to the Atlantic.

In 1936 British Prime Minister, Neville Chamberlain astounded and enraged Winston Churchill by agreeing with Eamon de Valera, Eire's Prime Minister, that its obligations in this matter would be allowed to lapse. Churchill, who had been First Lord of the Admiralty during WWI knew that such a concession could have serious consequences in the event of war.

Once Churchill became Prime Minister in 1940 he seriously considered reneging on Chamberlain's concession and placing the Royal Navy into the Treaty Ports regardless of de Valera's opinion. The down side was the anticipated antipathy generated in the Republic by such a cavalier move.

Britain was heavily dependant on Eire for food, a factor not to be taken lightly when it's supplies from the New World were being strangled by the U-boat war. It also benefitted greatly from Irish labour in its factories, hospitals and in the armed forces. Neither De Valera nor Hitler were in any doubt however, that if Churchill made up his mind to occupy the Treaty Ports, it would happen.

An uncomfortable gentleman's agreement ensued with Germany and Britain, more so, largely respecting Irish neutrality.

CHAPTER TEN
Kilmichael

If the Easter Rising of 1916 marked the beginning of Britain's troubles in 20th-Century Ireland, the Kilmichael ambush of November 1920 marked the beginning of the end for them. Nothing was ever the same again after a group of British Auxiliaries were ambushed and massacred on a lonely country road outside Dunmanway in West Cork. The Auxiliaries who might be termed 'Hooray Henrys' today, rampaged around the Irish countryside displaying an arrogance that had seen little colonial equal. After this and similar incidents the British Government began edging towards a treaty, eventually signed in 1922, that began the process of the withdrawal of British colonialism from southern Ireland after 600 years.

SS Irish Oak

The sinking of the Irish Oak in mid-Atlantic on 15 May 1943 by U-607 caused diplomatic exchanges and led to de Valera's return to power in the June 1943 elections but with a Fianna Fáil minority government. In the political smoke-screening that followed the finger of blame was pointed in every direction. The British suspected the Americans of sinking this neutral Irish merchant ship as 'punishment' for them not passing on information about German submarines. And *vice versa*.

There was also a call in the House of Commons for a formal protest to the Irish government because Irish Oak had not warned the convoy thirty miles ahead, of U-650 running alongside it, without communication, for several hours. The British government's response was that it had known of this U-boat's presence. De Valera insisted the Irish were not in the business of warning British convoys of German submarines. The Irish government and owners of the Irish Oak were also accused of supporting and operating Oak as a Q-ship, a heavily-armed merchantman designed to lure submarines to the surface so she might engage. This was also vigorously denied by both factions.

U-boat U-650 was not responsible for the Oak's demise by two torpedoes the following morning. The deed was done by U-607. It seems most likely the

Kriegsmarine were no longer tolerating neutral Irish ships, particularly the Irish Oak and her sister the SS Irish Pine (sunk on 16 November 1942 by U-608 with all hands lost), warning nearby convoys of their presence.

On 24 May 1943, Dönitz ordered the withdrawal of all U-boats from the Atlantic and the Battle of the Atlantic was over. Forty-one of these submarines had been lost in 'Black May' of 1943 alone, against the sinking of 50 allied ships.